EXPLORING SCOTLAND'S HERITAGE

Exploring Scotland's Heritage

ORKNEY AND SHETLAND

Anna Ritchie

The Royal Commission
on the Ancient and Historical Monuments
of Scotland

Edinburgh
Her Majesty's Stationery Office

Royal Commission on the Ancient and Historical Monuments of Scotland

John Sinclair House, 16 Bernard Terrace,
Edinburgh EH8 9NX (031-662 1456)

The Commission, which was established in 1908, is responsible for compiling a national record of archaeological sites and historic buildings of all types and periods. The Commission makes this record available both through its publications (details of which can be obtained from the above address) and through the maintenance of a central archive of information, known as the National Monuments Record of Scotland, which contains an extensive collection of pictorial and documentary material relating to Scotland's ancient monuments and historic buildings and is open daily for public reference.

Other titles in the series:
Argyll and the Western Isles
Lothian and the Borders
The Clyde Estuary and Central Region
Dumfries and Galloway
The Highlands
Grampian
Fife and Tayside

© Crown Copyright 1985
First Published 1985
Reprinted with minor revision 1993

ISBN 0 11 492458 9

CONTENTS

FOREWORD

Twentieth century Scotland has a heritage of human endeavour stretching back some nine thousand years, and a wide range of man-made monuments survives as proof of that endeavour. The rugged character of much of the Scottish landscape has helped to preserve many antiquities which elsewhere have vanished beneath modern development or intensive deep ploughing, though with some 3,850 km of coastline round mainland alone there has also been an immeasurable loss of archaeological sites as a result of marine erosion. Above all, perhaps, the preservation of such a wide range of monuments should be credited to Scotland's abundant reserves of good building stone, allowing not only the creation of extraordinarily enduring prehistoric houses and tombs but also the development of such remarkable Scottish specialities as the medieval tower-house and the iron-age broch. This volume is one of a series of eight handbooks which have been designed to provide up-to-date and authoritative introductions to the rich archaeological heritage of the various regions of Scotland, highlighting the most interesting and best preserved of the surviving monuments and setting them in their original social context. The time-scale is the widest possible, from relics of World War II or the legacy of 19th century industrial booms back through history and prehistory to the earliest pioneer days of human settlement, but the emphasis varies from region to region, matching the particular directions in which each has developed. Some monuments are still functioning (lighthouses for instance), others are still

occupied as homes, and many have been taken into the care of the State or the National Trust for Scotland, but each has been chosen as specially deserving a visit.

Thanks to the recent growth of popular interest in these topics, there is an increasing demand for knowledge to be presented in a readily digestible form and at a moderate price. In sponsoring this series, therefore, the Royal Commission on the Ancient and Historical Monuments of Scotland broadens the range of its publications with the aim of making authentic information about the man-made heritage available to as wide an audience as possible.

Monuments have been grouped according to their character and date and, although only the finest, most interesting or best preserved have been described in detail, attention has also been drawn to other sites worth visiting in the vicinity. Each section has its own explanatory introduction, beginning with the most recent monuments and gradually retreating in time back to the earliest traces of prehistoric man.

Each major monument is numbered and identified by its district so that it may easily be identified on the end-map, but it is recommended that the visitor should also use the relevant 1:50,000 maps published by the Ordnance Survey as its Landranger Series, particularly for the more remote sites. Sheet nos 5, 6 and 7 cover the Orkney Islands Area, and nos 1, 2, 3 and 4 cover the Shetland Islands Area. The National

Grid Reference for each site is provided (eg HP 629012) as well as local directions at the head of each entry.

An asterisk indicates that the site is subject to restricted hours of opening; unless attributed to Historic Buildings and Monuments: HBM(SDD), the visitor should assume the monument to be in private ownership and should seek permission locally to view it. It is of course vital that visitors to any monument should observe the country code and take special care to fasten gates. Where a church is locked, it is often possible to obtain the key from the local manse, post office or general store.

We have made an attempt to estimate how accessible each monument may be for disabled visitors, indicated at the head of each entry by a wheelchair logo and a number: 1=easy access for all visitors, including those in wheelchairs; 2=reasonable access for pedestrians but restricted access for wheelchairs; 3=restricted access for all disabled but a good view from the road or parking area; 4= access for the able-bodied only.

Many of the sites described in this guidebook are held in trust for the nation by the Secretary of State for Scotland and cared for on his behalf by Historic Buildings and Monuments, Scottish Development Department: HBM (SDD). Further information about these monuments, including publications, can be obtained from Historic Scotland, PO Box 157, Edinburgh EH3 5RA. Fair Isle is in the care of the National Trust for Scotland (NTS), and further information is available from the Trust, 5 Charlotte Square, Edinburgh EH2 4DR. The abbreviation RMS refers to the Royal Museum of Scotland, Queen Street, Edinburgh, whose collections include important material from the Northern Isles.

ANNA RITCHIE
Series Editor

ACKNOWLEDGMENTS

I should like to thank Dr Graham Ritchie for his patient help and encouragement during the preparation of this volume and Mr J G Dunbar for his kindness in reading and advising on the text. I am very grateful to Mr I F C Fleming for checking the National Grid references, to Mr I G Parker for preparing the maps and most of the line illustrations, and to Mrs Dorothy Baker for her impeccable typing. For advice and information I am indebted to Mr W F Ritchie, Mr Bryce Wilson, Dr Raymond Lamb and Mr and Mrs John Rendall on Orkney matters, and to Mr B Smith, Ms Val Turner, Mr A Williamson, Mr Ian Gow and Mr and Mrs Edwin Cope on Shetland matters. The inventory and archives of the Royal Commission on Ancient and Historical Monuments were an invaluable source of information; the lists of sites and monuments in several Orkney islands compiled by Dr Raymond Lamb gave valuable new insights. The assistance of Miss Audrey Henshall's important study of Scottish chambered tombs is gratefully acknowledged.

Many of the photographs and several line drawings were provided by the National Monuments Record for Scotland, Royal Commission on the Ancient and Historical Monuments of Scotland, including photographs taken by Dr G Ritchie, Dr R Lamb and the author. A number of photographs were kindly taken specially for this volume by M Brooks (pp. 10, 38, 42, 48, 55, 85, 94, 104, 126, 131, 141, 156, 168, 170) and D Wheeler (pp. 28, 30, 31), and their help is much appreciated. For the rest of the photographs, the author and the publisher are very grateful to the following institutions and individuals: Historic Buildings and Monuments (pp. 22, 23, 56, 71, 73, 74, 76, 78, 80, 81, 84, 86, 96, 97, 99, 100, 101, 102, 108, 109, 110, 111, 112, 113, 114, 115, 118, 119, 122, 132, 133, 134, 137, 140, 142, 146, 153, 156, 158, 159, 161, 162, 163, 164, 165); Royal Museum of Scotland, Queen Street, Edinburgh (pp. 13, 62, 95); Shetland Museum (p. 13); Scottish Record Office (p. 83, by kind permission of the Controller of HMSO); Aerofilms (p. 18); Dr A Whittle (p. 145); Dr J Hume (pp. 54, 62, 70); D Coutts (p. 116). Line drawings were kindly provided by T Borthwick (pp. 115, 161); I G Scott (pp. 129, 150); G D Hay (p.60); J Brandon-Jones (p. 46). Colour photographs were kindly provided by J Sowrey, including some taken specially for this book (opp. pp. 48, 64, 65); Dr G Ritchie (opp. pp. 49, 64, 65, 128, 129); M Brooks (opp. pp. 128, 129, 144, 145); the rest were taken by the author.

INTRODUCTION

Contrasts dominate the visitor's initial reaction to the Northern Isles. The physical appearances of Orkney and Shetland are quite different, and the contrasts between their traditional life-styles are reflected in their monuments to an extent that might suggest that the two island groups ought to be treated separately. Yet it is clear that, even from earliest times, their development was closely linked and that the contrasts are often superficial, masking an underlying unity, and for this reason their buildings and monuments will be discussed together in the following pages–although it is also hoped that the reader will gain an impression of the individual character not just of Orkney and Shetland as archipelagos but also of their component islands.

The physical contrast between the two archipelagos is explained by their geological formation: Orkney consists of sandstones and flagstones of the Old Red Sandstone series, giving rise to a gentle, even subdued landscape for the most part, whereas Shetland's rugged and diverse topography reflects a complex underlay including granites, schists and limestone as well as Old Red Sandstone formations. Nevertheless the contrast is incomplete, for Orkney displays stretches of wild and precipitous coastal scenery, especially along the western side of mainland and Hoy, and along the north-west perimeters of Rousay, Westray and Papa Westray. As a result of the rise in sea-level since the last ice age, both island groups are characterised by their drowned appearance, the long

sea inlets or voes of Shetland being partially submerged valleys and some of the Orkney islands rising so little above sea-level as to be a major hazard to ships. In geological terms, Orkney is an extension of Caithness, as might be expected with a stretch of sea only 10 km wide separating them, and the bleak landscape of western Hoy mirrors the austere upland moors of the Caithness interior, whereas Shetland compares more closely with the north-west Highlands of mainland Scotland.

Estimates of the number of islands in each group vary according to the criteria adopted; according to the British Geological Survey, Orkney consists of about 90 islands and skerries and Shetland of over 100 islands, although in both cases few of them are now inhabited. The major island in each group is known as mainland. Fair Isle, lying roughly half-way between Orkney and Shetland, belongs to the modern administrative area of Shetland, though it has in the past belonged to Orcadian landowners. A graphic impression of the physical difference between the Orkney and Shetland landscapes is conveyed by the fact that Shetland is not quite twice the size of Orkney (1426 sq km compared to 956 sq km) and yet has six times as long a coastline owing to its deeply indented voes. The sea is rarely out of sight and its influence immeasurable.

It is thought that Orkney was finally cut off by rising sea-levels from the mainland of Scotland around 11,000 BC and there followed a period of some seven

Ancient and modern in Noss Sound, Bressay: a ruined broch and a working croft

thousand years before the islands were colonised by man. The isolation of the islands had serious repercussions for early man, apart from the obvious effect that they could be reached only by sea: their fauna, and therefore their food resources, were very limited, for the larger mammals could not cross the Pentland Firth unaided. There could be no hunting, only fishing and fowling, and this explains why the Northern Isles remained uninhabited until the 4th millennium BC, by which time the economics of mixed farming had become a viable alternative to a life-style based on hunting and fishing. Neolithic farmers were accustomed to travelling with the young cattle and sheep and the seed corn necessary to their way of life—none of the wild prototypes were available in the British Isles—but in the case of Orkney and Shetland they had also to import deer and pigs. Once helped across the Pentland Firth, the deer would be able to swim to other islands within Orkney.

The task of transporting livestock and other commodities across the open sea in skin boats, log boats or on rafts is formidable in itself, but what is in retrospect truly astounding is the adventurous pioneering spirit that drove these people northwards. It was not necessary in the sense that land elsewhere was scarce. Nor were they foolhardy, for they seem only to have colonised visible horizons: Orkney is easily visible from Caithness, Fair Isle from Orkney, Shetland from Fair Isle. Away to the north-west and invisible even from Shetland, the Faroe Islands were to remain uninhabited for another 4000 years. In one respect, the Northern Isles were more attractive to settlement in early times than they are today: the climate was a little milder, sufficiently warm to grow not only barley but also wheat, and sea conditions more favourable for travel. More work has been done on the ancient environment in Orkney than in Shetland, but it is likely that conditions were similar; there is evidence to suggest that the earliest neolithic colonists encountered a landscape that included light woodland, mainly of birch and alder, but that by around 3000 BC the woodland had been largely replaced by open grassland and heath, the virtually treeless environment of today. The cause was a combination of several factors, most importantly an increase in wind-speed which led to plant-damage and coastal erosion and which was linked to an overall deterioration in the climate—the latter has continued with good patches and bad patches to the present day. It was a prolonged bad patch which led to the formation of a blanket of peat, a metre or more thick, over so much of Shetland and parts of Orkney towards the end of the 2nd millennium BC. Peat was to become an essential source of fuel but it obliterated large areas of formerly useful agricultural land.

The success of the early colonisation of the Northern Isles may be gauged from their funerary and ceremonial monuments even more than from their enduringly permanent settlements. The communities capable of sparing the labour and of organising the labour to build such colossal public monuments as the Ring of Brodgar in Orkney (no. 83) were living at an average standard far beyond that of mere subsistence. The earliest monuments are tombs, reflecting not only the importance of death and its associated ceremonies but also the origin of their builders: comparison of the design of tombs and of objects found in them indicates that Orkney and Shetland were settled by people who had lived previously in Caithness. There is no question of any contacts across the North Sea with Scandinavia, an orientation that was to become of paramount importance in Viking times; throughout their prehistory, the islands looked southwards into the rest of Britain for new ideas and influences. Nor is there evidence of any major influx of new blood between the original neolithic colonisation and the Viking settlement in the 9th century AD, although it is equally unlikely that the population remained entirely static—despite their location at the northern extremity of Britain, the Northern Isles participated in the same overall technological and ideological development as the rest of the country.

The level of participation has, however, varied, and this is particularly evident in early prehistoric times. During the first half of the 3rd millennium, Orkney was so firmly in the mainstream of developments that it shared the same material culture as communities in southern England: the same pottery and tools, the same great ceremonial monuments known to us as henges. Thereafter a degree of insularity may be seen throughout the 2nd millennium, when the new fashions in pottery and particularly in metal working were only barely felt in the Northern Isles. The strength of their material resources lay in stone: flagstone for building, steatite for bowls, loom-weights, line-sinkers and other equipment, felsite for sharp-bladed knives. The new bronze technology depended upon copper ore, of which Orkney and Shetland had little available to prehistoric man (the copper-bearing veins exploited in the 19th century at Sand Lodge in Shetland had to be mined), and tin, which had to be imported from Cornwall. All this combined to make bronze an expensive commodity, and bronze jewellery and tools are rare finds. New ideas in burial customs were adopted, however, with individual burials, often cremated, under mounds replacing the stone chambered tombs of earlier times.

Northern fortunes revived and trading horizons widened again from around 500 BC into historical times, most clearly reflected in the architectural record by the stone-built forts known as brochs, which physically dominated the land and seascapes of Orkney and Shetland in the last couple of centuries BC and the first couple of centuries AD. The broch was a design shared with like-minded communities in northern and western Scotland, for whom protection of life and chattels was clearly a necessity in what must have been aggressive times. The same social conditions elsewhere in Britain and Europe were met by massive hillforts, and the broch should be seen as a parallel form of local response (rather than as a refuge against Roman slave-ships as sometimes claimed).

Although the Romans knew of the Northern Isles, and Roman goods reached the islands; the Roman military presence in southern Scotland had no direct effect there. When the Roman general, Agricola, sent his fleet on an exploratory voyage round the north of Britain in AD 84, it is likely that they passed between Orkney and Shetland, the islands they knew as the *Orcades* and *Thule*. Perhaps the most important effect of Roman activities in Scotland was on local politics in stimulating the tribal unification that led ultimately to the creation of the kingdom of the Picts in the 6th century AD, but there is no means of estimating the involvement of the Northern Isles in this process nor of evaluating their status in the kingdom. Combining the archaeological evidence with the few historical references, there is no doubt that both Orkney and Shetland were part of Pictland, but it seems likely that they may have retained some political autonomy. During this period, from the 6th century AD until the Viking onslaught around 800 put an end to any political affiliations with mainland Scotland south of the Moray Firth, the islands were converted to Christianity.

The geographical setting of the islands took on a new significance with the beginning of the Viking age. The fact that it is the same distance from Lerwick to Bergen as from Lerwick to Aberdeen was irrelevant before the development of sea-going craft capable of crossing the North Sea at this latitude, and it was their ships and seamanship that allowed the Vikings to dominate the western seaways. The advantages of colonising Orkney and Shetland were many and obvious, both for their own economic value as estates for landless Norsemen and for their nodal position on the route between Norway and the riches to be looted in Ireland, and the Picts were obliged to accept, in the course of the 9th and 10th centuries, the creation of a powerful Norse earldom. A variety of monuments testifies to the economic success of the earldom—farms, cemeteries, churches—but the real proof lies in the density of Scandinavian placenames, all but obliterating earlier indigenous names and demonstrating that the Norsemen intended to superimpose their own culture, language and customs. A few island names of native origin were retained (eg Unst, Yell), but most names are firmly Scandinavian, helpfully indicating the homelands of the settlers as well as charting the spread of Norse settlement in the islands. The settlers came from the west coast of Norway, and many of the names that they bestowed upon Orkney and Shetland were names with which they were familiar in Norway, names appropriate to the topography of the land: Sandwick, sand bay; Lerwick, mud bay; ness, headland. Many farm-names contain the basic Scandinavian generic terms, *stathr*, dwelling-place or farm, *setr*, dwelling, *bólstathr*, farm, as in Gunnista, Mossetter, Kirbuster. The blanket effect of Scandinavian placenames was so effective and enduring that, aside from replacing earlier names, they left little opportunity for later Scottish naming. The modern dialects of Shetland and Orkney contain many Scots words, in many cases fossilised 16th century Scots words adopted during a period of maximum immigration from lowland Scotland or farming terms reflecting the influx into Orkney in the 19th century of farmers from north-east Scotland, but placenames have remained essentially Scandinavian.

Particularly confusing in an archaeological context are the modern terms arising from Old Norse *borg*, fort, which can occur as burg or brough with its literal meaning of fort or as brough meaning a promontory almost or entirely detached from mainland like the Brough of Birsay in Orkney. A group of placenames of special interest is that containing the element *papar*, of which sixteen examples occur in the Northern Isles, two in Caithness, nine in the Western Isles and none in the rest of Scotland. It is clear from early Norse documentary sources that *papar* was the name given to Irish hermits in Iceland and that there are equivalent *papar* placenames in Iceland, and the fact that such placenames do not occur in Ireland itself, or on the Scottish mainland other than Caithness in the far north, implies that the name was invented by Norsemen and used to describe places associated with monks and hermits; places that were usually islands or remote coastal areas: eg Papa Westray and Papa Stronsay in Orkney, Papil on West Burra, Papil Geo on the island of Noss and Papa Stour in Shetland. In Iceland, *papi* is a nickname for the puffin, and it seems that pagan Norsemen regarded both puffins and religious men as faintly ridiculous—and that *papar* placenames might refer to the presence of either (or indeed both, as they tended to choose the same sort of precipitous places to live). The cross-slab from Papil churchyard on West Burra includes two bird-men amongst its decorative motifs; they appear to have been added to the cross-slab by a different stone-carver, and it has been suggested that they are the work of an irreverent Norseman, portraying his idea of puffin-clerics. Looking at the rotund cloaked and hooded clerics on the Monks' Stone from Papil, one can appreciate their resemblance to puffins!

The political history of the Northern Isles is documented only from the foundation of the Norse earldom in the 9th century AD, its fortunes recorded in several Icelandic sagas but primarily in *Orkneyinga Saga*, a record compiled around AD 1200 by an Icelandic historian whose name is now lost but who

Monks' Stone from Papil, West Burra

Cross-slab from Papil, West Burra

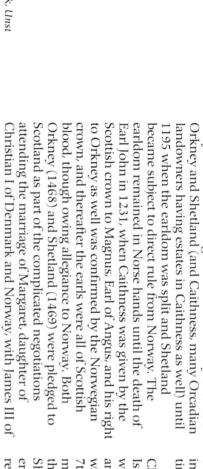

Burgar stack, Unst

was more familiar with events, families and places in Orkney than in Shetland. It is a fascinating piece of early historical writing. The earls held sway over both Orkney and Shetland (and Caithness, many Orcadian landowners having estates in Caithness as well) until 1195 when the earldom was split and Shetland became subject to direct rule from Norway. The earldom remained in Norse hands until the death of Earl John in 1231, when Caithness was given by the Scottish crown to Magnus, Earl of Angus, and his right to Orkney as well was confirmed by the Norwegian crown, and thereafter the earls were all of Scottish blood, though owing allegiance to Norway. Both Orkney (1468) and Shetland (1469) were pledged to Scotland as part of the complicated negotiations attending the marriage of Margaret, daughter of Christian I of Denmark and Norway, with James III of Scotland. From then on, the Northern Isles were administered together by the Scottish crown, although their links with Norway remained strong, particularly in trade and the essential importing of Norwegian timber for boat-building.

Christianity was certainly established in the Northern Isles by the 8th century AD, but precisely how and when it was first introduced are difficult questions to answer. The Pictish kingdom on mainland Scotland was converted gradually during the late 6th and 7th centuries by St Columba and the Irish missionaries who followed him, and it is likely that their work extended northwards to Orkney and Shetland. At the same time it seems that small eremitic monasteries were being established on remote headlands and offshore stacks by Irish ascetics, who would not themselves engage in missionary activities. Several of these monastic settlements survive with visible traces of the small cells in which the hermits lived, but they are as inaccessible today as 1300 years ago; an example illustrated here is a stack site at Burgar on Unst in Shetland (HP 661139).

By the 8th century there was also strong influence from Northumbria through the established Pictish Church, seen most clearly in the art of the stone carver; the exquisite eagle carved on the symbol stone from the Knowe of Burrian on mainland Orkney bears a very close relationship to the eagle used in Northumbrian illustrated gospels as the evangelical symbol of St John (this stone is now in THM). Apart from sculpture, very little evidence survives on the ground of the early Church in the Northern Isles, though fragments of carved stone shrines from St Ninian's Isle (no. 47) and from Papil on Burra, Shetland, give a tantalising glimpse of the interiors of lost chapels. A slab carved with a beautiful, interlace-filled cross is all that survives of an 8th century church on the island of Flotta, Orkney; it was probably the front panel of a stone-built altar (RMS).

According to saga evidence, the Norse earldom of Orkney and Shetland was obliged to accept Christianity in 995 by the Norwegian king, Olaf Tryggvason, who promised death and devastation as the only alternative, but in fact the Norse conversion began in the 9th century under Pictish influence and was a gradual process. It is reflected in early Scandinavian settlement names containing the Old Norse element *kirkja*, church, eg Kirbister, and by the fact that the pagan tradition of burial with personal gravegoods was being replaced by unaccompanied Christian burial during the 10th century. This is seen very clearly in the Norse family cemetery at Westness on Rousay (see the Rousay excursion), where both pagan and Christian graves have been excavated.

The bishopric of Orkney and Shetland was founded in the 11th century, but its character was missionary rather than formally residential until around 1160, when the bishop's seat was established at Birsay. Once the building of St Magnus Cathedral was underway in Kirkwall, the bishops resided there and the episcopal complex at Birsay was abandoned. Initially the bishopric was associated with the Archbishoprics of Hamburg-Bremen and York, but from about 1112 it came under the Archbishop of Lund and from 1153 it was transferred to the new province of Nidaros (Trondheim). Scandinavian and particularly Norwegian influence on ecclesiastical architecture was thus strong, but so was Anglo-Norman influence in Scandinavia, with the result that stylistic influences cannot be compartmentalised too strictly. Even after the earldom of Orkney and Shetland was split in 1195, the islands remained in the same bishopric, its clergy mostly Norwegian until the later 15th century when Scots became increasingly dominant. In 1472 the bishopric was transferred to the see of St Andrews. The ancient connection with Nidaros was commemorated in 1937 by the gift from the Church of Norway to St Magnus Cathedral of a replica of the statue of St Olaf at Nidaros Cathedral.

Once Christianity had been accepted by leading Norse families, there was a building period in the 12th century during which many small chapels were constructed to serve family estates, and Orkney and Shetland are fortunate in the number of these that have survived. It is usually, but not always, the chapels which did not become parish churches that remain, ruinous but little altered, whereas parish churches underwent modification or re-building. Considerable impetus to this 12th century building programme must have been provided by the immense project going on in Kirkwall, the creation of St Magnus Cathedral, which began in 1137. As the relics of St Magnus were to be housed in this new cathedral, perhaps it was local pride that prompted the building of a new church on Egilsay where the saint had been murdered.

The cathedral apart, the medieval churches of the Northern Isles were simple unpretentious structures which did not incur the wrath of the 1560 Scottish Reformation. Nor were there rich monasteries to punish, although it may not be a coincidence that the medieval monastery on Eynhallow (no. 52) appears to have been secularised in the 16th century. Even St Magnus Cathedral survived the Reformation unscathed, though it had a narrow escape at the hands of the Earl of Caithness in 1614 during the insurrection of Robert Stewart.

The later 15th and 16th centuries witnessed frequent power struggles between the ruling families of the Northern Isles and the Scottish crown, and the political turbulence of the period is reflected in its buildings. The development of Kirkwall was closely linked with royal efforts to curb the power of the Sinclairs in the late 15th century, for the town was made a royal burgh in 1486 and it was given possession of the cathedral as a counter-measure against the Sinclairs' advantage in owning the castle in Kirkwall, the cathedral being the only large defensible building comparable to the castle. The cathedral

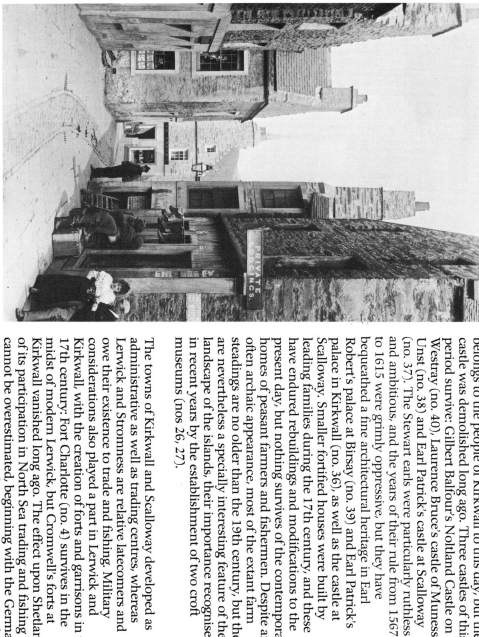

belongs to the people of Kirkwall to this day, but the castle was demolished long ago. Three castles of this period survive: Gilbert Balfour's Noltland Castle on Westray (no. 40), Laurence Bruce's castle of Muness on Unst (no. 38) and Earl Patrick's castle at Scalloway (no. 37). The Stewart earls were particularly ruthless and ambitious, and the years of their rule from 1567 to 1615 were grimly oppressive, but they have bequeathed a fine architectural heritage in Earl Robert's palace at Birsay (no. 39) and Earl Patrick's palace in Kirkwall (no. 36), as well as the castle at Scalloway. Smaller fortified houses were built by leading families during the 17th century, and these have endured rebuildings and modifications to the present day, but nothing survives of the contemporary homes of peasant farmers and fishermen. Despite an often archaic appearance, most of the extant farm steadings are no older than the 19th century, but they are nevertheless a specially interesting feature of the landscape of the islands, their importance recognised in recent years by the establishment of two croft museums (nos 26, 27).

The towns of Kirkwall and Scalloway developed as administrative as well as trading centres, whereas Lerwick and Stromness are relative latecomers and owe their existence to trade and fishing. Military considerations also played a part in Lerwick and Kirkwall, with the creation of forts and garrisons in the 17th century: Fort Charlotte (no. 4) survives in the midst of modern Lerwick, but Cromwell's forts at Kirkwall vanished long ago. The effect upon Shetland of its participation in North Sea trading and fishing cannot be overestimated, beginning with the German and Dutch merchants of the Hanseatic League in the 15th and 16th centuries and culminating in the great days of the herring fishing in the late 19th and early 20th centuries, of which the merchant's booth on Whalsay (no. 9) and the harbour fronts at Stromness (no. 11) and Lerwick (no. 12) are tangible reminders. Nor was the strategic importance of Shetland and Orkney confined to their fishing grounds, for they became vital bases during the wars of the 19th and 20th centuries. Like the herring fishing, wartime brought a temporary influx of vast numbers of people—the impact on Orcadian economy of the Second World War has been described as 'some monstrous tourist bonanza', for it created a captive market of thousands of servicemen. The ruins of many military and naval installations may still be seen, and it is not difficult to appreciate the wartime importance of the anchorages in Scapa Flow and Bressay Sound.

Until as recently as 300 years ago, there were no marine charts to guide shipping round the hazardous coasts of the Northern Isles, and navigation depended upon personal experience and knowledge of coastal waters. The Pentland Firth is particularly dangerous: in the days of sailing ships it was known as 'hell's mouth' because of the ferocious eddies and tidal races, and many ships preferred the longer route round the north of Orkney. Innumerable local hazards make the coasts of both Orkney and Shetland very treacherous, from the 'roost' or *dynrost* (so called from the awful noise of its turbulent waters) off Sumburgh Head to the sometimes invisible island of Sanday, so low and flat as to escape notice in a high sea. With the growth of the fishing industry in the 17th and 18th centuries, the need for lighthouses became imperative, and the first lights provided in the Northern Isles were those on North Ronaldsay and the Pentland Skerries in Orkney, built at the end of the 18th century, and Sanday in Orkney and Sumburgh Head in Shetland in the early 19th century.

Throughout the 19th century, the Northern Lighthouse Board was served by engineers from the Stevenson family, and it was in the company of Robert Stevenson and the commissioners of the Northern Lights in 1814 that Sir Walter Scott made his famous voyage around Scotland. In the journal that he kept (recently republished as *Northern Lights*), Sir Walter describes a visit to see the newly built lighthouse on Sanday in which he was struck by the high standard of the keepers' living quarters: 'All in excellent order and the establishment of the keepers in the same style of comfort and respectability as elsewhere—far better than the house of the master of the Fair Isle and rivalling my own baronial mansion of Abbotsford.' One is left wondering if he really approved of such comforts!

The history and development of the Northern Isles over the last five and half thousand years are well illustrated by a wide range of stone buildings and earthworks; some conform to fashions widespread beyond the islands, demonstrating that their peripheral geographical location was rarely matched by any cultural isolation, while others have a special interest as examples of man's response to local conditions of climate or resources. The similarities and the contrasts between Orkney and Shetland are equally striking, but together or separately the two island groups repay exploration with a remarkable insight into their past.

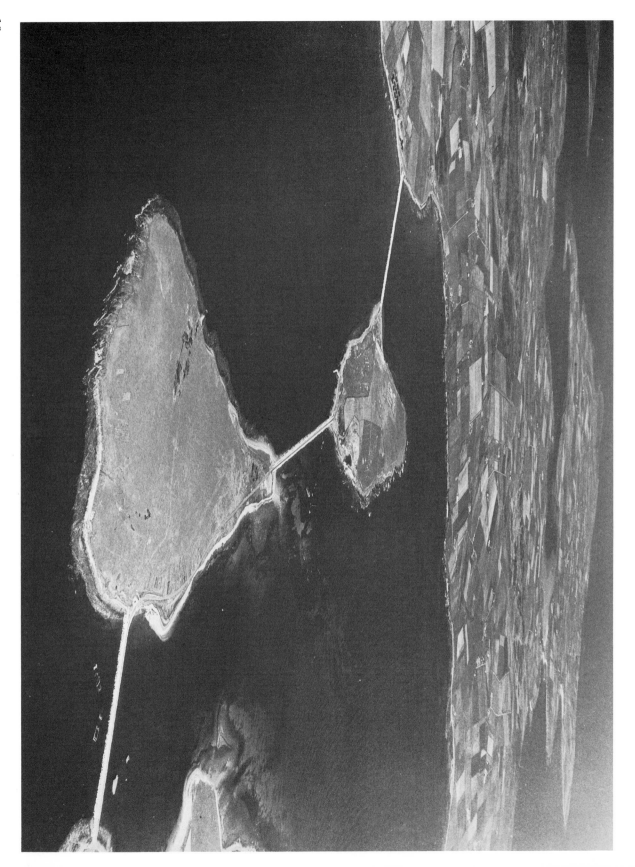

1

MILITARY ARCHITECTURE AND LIGHTHOUSES

The Northern Isles hold a special attraction for visitors with an interest in military and naval warfare. Fort Charlotte at Lerwick, begun in 1665, is a rare and well-preserved survivor of the series of forts of geometric design initiated in Scotland under Cromwell's rule and culminating in the mid 18th century in the remarkable military achievement of Fort George, Inverness-shire (unfortunately nothing is visible today of the two forts built by Cromwell at Kirkwall). Fort Charlotte was built originally against Dutch aggression in the 17th century, but it received substantial reconstruction in 1781, again as a result of hostilities with Holland during the American War of Independence, and it was then that the fort at Lerwick was re-named after Queen Charlotte.

When Sir Walter Scott visited Orkney in 1814, he saw in progress the construction of a remarkable military installation at Longhope on the south-east extremity of Hoy. This was the Longhope battery with its attendant twin martello towers of Hackness (no. 3) and Crockness (ND 324934), built to safeguard the Longhope anchorage during the war with the United States of America that had begun in 1812. Longhope was unusual on several counts, not least because it turned out to be a white elephant. Longhope was an essential but highly vulnerable anchorage: essential because it offered shelter from all winds adjacent to the treacherous Pentland Firth and yet was served by four sea approaches between islands, and vulnerable because there was no land-based defence against sea-

borne marauders who could decimate the ships at anchor like penned-in sheep. During the American war, Longhope was adopted as the rendezvous anchorage for trading ships bound for the Baltic, which waited for the naval warship that would escort the convoy across the North Sea. They presented a sitting target for the American privateers and the need for their defence was acknowledged and met by the provision of guns mounted on a standard battery and backed up by others mounted on the two martello towers.

The name martello and the idea of such towers had been adopted by Britain after experience of them in Corsica at the end of the 18th century; martello is a corruption of the name of Cape Mortella in Corsica, where English forces captured one of these towers in 1794. With their height and thick walls, martello towers provided an excellent defence against attack from the sea, and no fewer than 103 were built along south-eastern English coasts against the threat of a Napoleonic invasion from France in 1803-5. The invasion threat continued even after the Battle of Trafalgar in 1805, and led to the construction of a martello tower to guard Leith harbour at Edinburgh in 1809 (Longhope and Leith were the only such towers to be built in Scotland).

In the event, the American war was over and Napoleon finally overthrown before the Longhope battery and martello towers were completed; even during the war

The Churchill Barriers between St Mary's Holm, Lamb Holm, Glims Holms and Burray (no. 1)

no American privateer had attempted to attack a convoy at anchorage, preferring to swoop on the open sea. The towers were refurbished to take modern gun mountings in 1866, along with extensive modification of the battery, in response to the threat of Irish-American privateers, but again the threat failed to materialise and the Longhope guns remained silent. In fact, they were never fired in anger. Just once, in 1892, the 68-pounder cannons at Longhope were fired as a peaceful exercise by the Orkney Artillery Volunteers, but they were long obsolete by the First World War.

Orkney, especially the anchorage at Scapa Flow, played an important part in both great wars with Germany in the early 20th century, primarily because of her strategic position for intercepting enemy ships bound for the Atlantic but also, in 1939, Orkney was thought to be outside the range of German torpedo-carrying aircraft and therefore a safe base for the British Home Fleet. There are many structural traces of the two wars, from the absurd 'Burma Road' built as a military exercise in the early 1940s and leading to a roundabout in the middle of nowhere (HY 593083) to the batteries lining the shores of Scapa Flow and the disused airfields such as that at Twatt, Birsay. Among the most notable relics of the 1914-18 war are the blockships sunk to deter enemy submarines entering Scapa Flow through the eastern approaches, especially those blocking Holm Sound between the islands of Lamb Holm, Glims Holm and Burray. On Marwick

Head at Birsay, there is a large memorial to the war hero Lord Kitchener and his men, drowned when the HMS *Hampshire* was sunk by a mine on June 5, 1916; the square castellated tower was erected by the people of Orkney in 1926 (HY 226251).

On the east side of Shetland, the shelter of Swarbacks Minn between Vementry and Muckle Roe was used as an advance base for the Scapa Flow fleet, and a rare survival from the First World War may be seen on the small island of Vementry, in the form of gun emplacements guarding the entry to Swarbacks Minn. Not only the bunkers and hut foundations survive on Swarbacks Head but also two six-inch guns (HU 290619).

The safeguarding of Scapa Flow was again of vital importance in World War Two, highlighted in October 1939 by the sinking of the *Royal Oak* battleship by a German U-boat that managed to squeeze in past the old blockships. This time the eastern approaches were sealed permanently by the Churchill Barriers, solid obstacles composed of concrete blocks and created by the labour of Italian prisoners-of-war (no. 1). The other marine defences have gone, the booms, mine loops and anti-submarine nets, but the Barriers remain, as road-bearing causeways linking the southern isles—and as the most recent, standing historical monuments of the Northern Isles with which this volume is concerned.

1 Churchill Barriers, Orkney ♿

AD 1941-3.

HY 483012-ND 476948. Foundations for sections of the A 961 between St Mary's Holm and St Margaret's Hope, South Ronaldsay.

There are four barriers spanning the sounds between mainland, Lamb Holm, Glims Holm, Burray and South Ronaldsay, a total length of some 2.3 km. They were built during the Second World War with the object of blocking the four eastern approaches to Scapa Flow, as part of an attempt to create a safe anchorage for the British Home Fleet. Massive concrete blocks were made and set in position by Italian prisoners-of-war and, after the war, the barriers were surfaced as a foundation for the modern road. The predecessors of the barriers, the block-ships sunk during the First World War for the same strategic purpose, can be seen alongside.

The first stage in the construction of the barriers was to lay down a rubble base: in some places the water was up to 18 m deep, and it took a quarter of a million tons of stone and rubble to complete the foundation, most of it from a quarry on Lamb Holm. The casting yard for the concrete blocks was at St Mary's Holm, where some 66,000 blocks were made, weighing five or ten tons each, and these were laid on top of the rubble base. The barriers also provide an insight into the results of human intervention in the natural environment, because over the four decades since they were built there has been a massive accumulation of sand against them.

The Churchill Barrier between St Mary's Holm and Lamb Holm (no. 1)

Hackness martello tower, Hoy (no. 3)

2 Italian Chapel, Lamb Holm, Orkney

AD 1943-5.
HY 488006. Signposted footpath E from A 961.

The ingenuity and improvisation of the Italian prisoners-of-war who had worked on the Churchill Barriers led to the creation of this small chapel dedicated to *Regina Pacis*, the Queen of Peace. It was designed by Domenico Chiocchetti, an artist and church decorator in peacetime, and consists of two Nissen huts placed end-to-end with embellishments made largely from materials salvaged from the sea: the entrance has an elaborate facade with pinnacles and a bellcote, and the colourful interior has been kept impeccably. The prisoner-of-war camp was already abandoned by the time that the chapel was finished in 1945, and the first sung mass was delayed until 1959.

3 Hackness Martello Tower and Battery, Hoy, Orkney

AD 1815 and 1866.
ND 338912. At the NE end of the South Walls peninsula, side road off the B 9047.
HBM (SDD).

The tower appears to be circular, but the wall on the seaward side is twice as thick as that on the landward side in order to withstand bombardment, and this creates an elliptical plan. Inside, each of the floors is circular. Access into the tower is on the landward side at first-floor level, as a defensive measure; a single doorway, set at a height of about 4 m above ground-level and reached originally by a portable ladder, leads into the living quarters for the gunners and their N.C.O. The tower had its own water-supply from a cistern built into the foundations, and the water could be raised to the living quarters by a hand-pump set into the recess on the left-hand side of the entrance passage. The beds were arranged radially round the wall, and the N.C.O. had the privacy of his own cubicle. Stairs within the thickness of the wall led down to the ground-level storeroom and magazine and up to the parapet and gun platform. At a height of some 10 m above the ground, the top of the tower gives a wide view over the approaches to the Longhope anchorage, and the 24-pounder cannon could also guard the landward side of the battery against any attack from a landing party. The original gun mounting was modified in 1866, and the tower was used as a naval signal-post during the First World War.

Less than 180 m to the north-west of the tower lies the battery, designed as a powerful deterrent with eight 24-pounder guns sweeping the south-east approaches to Longhope through Switha Sound and Cantick Sound. The gunners were protected by a stone parapet and an embankment, while behind the battery were their barracks and stores and a magazine built partially underground, the whole installation enclosed within a high stone wall on the landward side. Most important of the extensive renovations carried out in 1866 was the remodelling of the battery itself to provide heavier guns and better protection for the gunners: four 68-pounder cannons were mounted so as to fire through embrasures rather than simply over the parapet. Additional domestic buildings include, beside the gate, an officers' block which later became a farmhouse. The sandstone used to build both the Hackness and Crockness martello towers and the battery was quarried at Bring Head on the north-east coast of Hoy and transported by boat to Longhope.

*Hackness martello tower, Hoy:
gun mounting and parapet (no. 3)*

Hackness battery, Hoy (no. 3)

Aerial view of Fort Charlotte, Lerwick: (no. 4)

4 Fort Charlotte, Lerwick, Shetland

17th and 18th century AD.
HU 475415. Within the N part of the town, overlooking the harbour.
HBM (SDD).

The substantial remains of this impressive fort have been surrounded by modern Lerwick, but, when it was built in the 17th century, it stood isolated and forbidding on a cliff to the north of the village, with its gun-ports looming over Bressay Sound. Because its fire-power had to be concentrated along its east side, the plan of the fort is less regularly geometric on plan than was normal; it is roughly pentagonal, with a massive seaward wall which is angled rather than straight in order to increase the range of the nine gun-ports massed along it. Each of the five bastions set at the angles of the rest of the fort-wall was also provided

with gun-ports, up to a maximum of five in the west bastion. Although the building of the fort began in 1665 (designed by no less a man than John Mylne, Master Mason to King Charles II), it was burnt by the Dutch in 1673 and lay in disrepair for more than a century until 1782 when it was renovated by the Chief Engineer for North Britain and renamed Fort Charlotte in honour of the Queen. The 18th century fort had three gates, with the main gate between the west and south-west bastions, and a gun-track led from the north gate out to the Knab headland, the first formal road to be built in Shetland. Within the fort, on three sides of a central parade-ground, were built accommodation blocks: the main west block provided barracks for the garrison, with officers' quarters in the projecting bays at either end, the north block consisted of ground-level kitchen and stores and first-floor accommodation for the Commanding Officer, and the south block held guard-rooms and artillery stores.

Fort Charlotte, Lerwick: west and north barrack blocks (no. 4)

Fort Charlotte, Lerwick: south gate (no. 4)

LIGHTHOUSES

Start Point lighthouse, Sanday, by W Daniell, 1821 (no. 5)

Measures designed to improve safety at sea have created a range of monuments from major lighthouses to unlit beacons and even cairns of stones that act as navigational markers. Orkney possesses eleven major lighthouses and Shetland has seven, each consisting of a circular tower to carry the light and low ranges of keepers' accommodation; the latter can be architecturally as interesting as the towers themselves. Bressay (HU 488376), built in 1858 to guide ships into Lerwick, has two fine blocks of living quarters, while

Hoy High (HY 268060), one of the two lighthouses built on Graemsay in 1851, can boast of keepers' houses built in an impressive style that has been likened to Assyrian temples.

Sumburgh Head, notorious for its shipwrecks, received its lighthouse in 1821 (HU 407078), but the equally notorious Fair Isle coast remained unlit until the end of the century. Concern for the safety of Royal Navy ships prompted one of the most difficult of all British lighthouse-building projects on the rock-stack of Muckle Flugga, Unst, in 1854 (HP 606196). By the end of the 19th century, minor, unmanned lights were becoming common, each with a local attendant keeper who paid twice-weekly visits to maintain the light and consisting of little more than a tower—that on the Brough of Birsay, Orkney (HY 234285), built in 1925, is worth visiting in conjunction with earlier monuments on the island (see no. 57).

The lighthouses on North Ronaldsay and Sanday present between them a fascinating visual impression of the way in which early lights developed. The tower on Dennis Head, North Ronaldsay (no. 7), was one of the first four lights built by the Northern Lighthouse Board (the others were on the Mull of Kintyre in Argyll, Eilean Glas on Harris and Kinnaird Head in Aberdeenshire); these early lights had fixed lanterns consisting of a mass of individual lamps each with its own reflector, burning whale oil. The original tower on Start Point, Sanday (no. 5), had no lantern and was only of daytime use, but in 1806 it was fitted with an innovatory 'revolving' light, in which the reflector frame revolved by clockwork mechanism. Previously the only way to achieve light visible from more than one direction was to build double lights with twin towers as on the Pentland Skerries, and the new revolving light was less expensive to maintain. Start Point was so successful that the light on Dennis Head was abandoned.

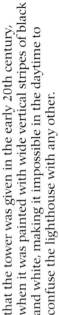

5 Start Point, Lighthouse, Sanday, Orkney

19th century AD.

HY 786435. Start Point is a tidal island at the E tip of Sanday and the lighthouse, although clearly visible from the mainland, can be reached only at low tide on foot across the sand.

The original tower was built in 1802 as an unlit beacon and converted into a revolving light in 1806, but it was rebuilt in brick in 1870. The tower is just over 22 m high and the light was made automatic in 1962. The original keepers' accommodation admired by Sir Walter Scott has survived in good condition alongside the towers; the proportions and overall design of the house and the original tower were particularly fine. Perhaps the most remarkable aspect of the modern lighthouse is the distinctive marking that the tower was given in the early 20th century, when it was painted with wide vertical stripes of black and white, making it impossible in the daytime to confuse the lighthouse with any other.

6 Dennis Head, Lighthouse, North Ronaldsay, Orkney

AD 1854.

HY 784559. Still manned; at the end of track leading across Dennis Ness from main road. Northern Lighthouse Board.

A new lighthouse was built on North Ronaldsay in 1854, almost a kilometre to the north-west of the old beacon. Dennis Ness is so low and flat that an exceptionally tall tower was needed: at a height of 41 m, this is the tallest land-based lighthouse built in the British Isles. In common with other lighthouses built at a similar period, the tower was constructed of red brick rather than stone as an economy measure, and the bricks had to be imported. The tower was given its two broad white bands of paint in 1889 in order to distinguish it in daylight.

7 Dennis Head, Lighthouse, North Ronaldsay, Orkney

AD 1789.

HY 790553. On SE tip of Dennis Head, less than 0.5 km walk over rough pasture from the road near Bewan.

The oldest lighthouse in the Northern Isles, this is a very pleasing stone-built tower some 21 m high. It was built in 1789 as a manned light, but in 1809 it was converted into an unlit beacon and the lantern was replaced by a great ball of masonry which had topped the beacon at Start Point, Sanday.

The tower survives in good condition externally, but the timber stairs inside have rotted away; the ruins of the original keepers' house may be seen alongside.

Dennis Head lighthouse, North Ronaldsay (no. 7)

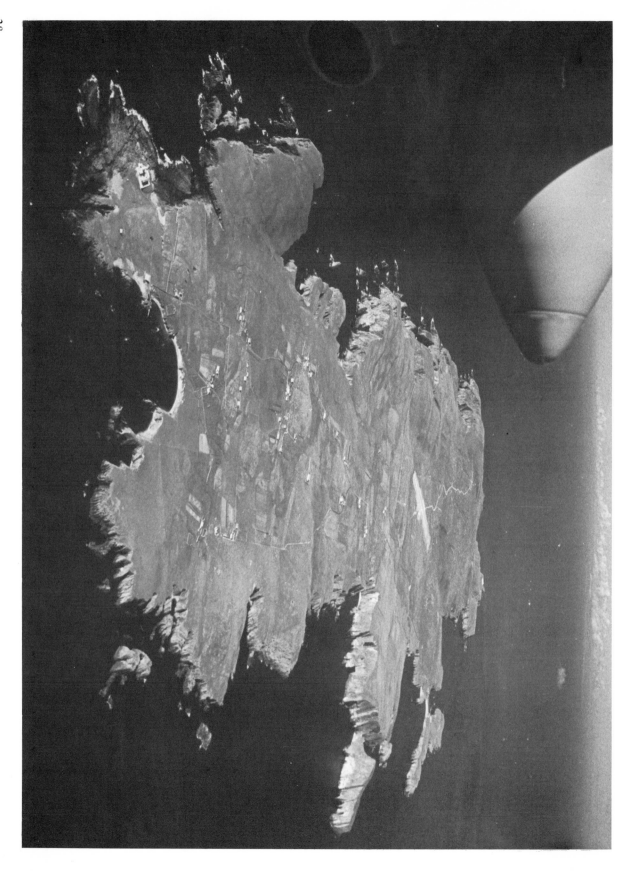

2

FAIR ISLE

Fair Isle was inhabited in prehistoric times, but the name by which we know it was bestowed by Vikings, to whom the island was a familiar sight on their voyages between Norway, the Northern Isles and the west coast of Scotland. *Fritharey* (peaceful isle) they called it, and it is a fair island, even though living there has never been easy. It lies roughly halfway between Orkney and Shetland, and, although in modern administrative terms the island is part of Shetland, in the past it has been owned both by Shetlanders and Orcadians. Since 1954, Fair Isle has belonged to the National Trust for Scotland, who have successfully developed a crofting programme for the islanders as well as the world-famous Bird Observatory: the study of breeding birds and an extraordinary range of migrant birds is one of the island's major attractions for visitors.

Fair Isle is made up of sedimentary rocks of Middle Old Red Sandstone age, and their formation slopes very steeply to the south-east; this has created a very rugged and beautiful coastline of steep cliffs and rock stacks, particularly on the west coast where the deep geos have been carved by the sea along fault-lines in the rock. There is of course another side to the beauty of such a coastline: combined with the strong currents that beset the island, Fair Isle has been the cause of a great number of shipwrecks, from famous sailing ships of centuries past to long forgotten fishing boats. It was presumably this aspect of the island that prompted German air-borne attacks on both lighthouses in World War II.

Fair Isle waters contain one of the most famous of all Shetland wrecks, a ship of the Spanish Armada which, having barely survived battle with English ships in the English Channel, finally sank at Stronshellier on the south-east coast of Fair Isle on 28 September 1588. *El Gran Grifon* was a hired store ship, a 650 ton merchantman acting as the flagship for the Armada's squadron of supply ships, and it is said that, during the battle, she sustained forty direct hits in her hull from English guns. After its defeat, the Armada sailed northwards and ran into appalling gales and heavy seas; half the fleet foundered and the rest scattered, attempting to return home to Spain round the north of Britain. A vivid account of the final days of *El Gran Grifon* survives in Spanish in a diary kept by one of her sailors: a struggle against the elements in which attempts failed either to sail westwards between Orkney and Shetland or to flee east to Norway. Nor was it possible to land on any of the northern isles of Orkney in such perilous seas. Ultimately the ship managed to anchor off Fair Isle, and it appears to have sunk during an attempt to beach. Three hundred of her sailors and officers scrambled to safety, but food on Fair Isle was in such short supply that fifty died of starvation over the following six weeks before rescue could be summoned from the mainland of Shetland. The writer of the diary was clearly taken aback at the low standard of living on Fair Isle: he describes them as 'a very dirty people, neither Christians nor altogether heretics', who were living in 'huts more like hovels than anything else' and using as fuel a

29

Fair Isle, north lighthouse

substance totally alien to a Spaniard, peat. There were only seventeen families, amounting probably to less than a hundred people, who must have been equally aghast at the sudden arrival of three hundred uninvited guests!

Despite its history of shipwrecks, Fair Isle had no lighthouse until 1892 when two were built, one at the northern tip of the island (HZ 22174) and one at the south end (HZ 197698); the North Light is still manned. The location of the island between Orkney and Shetland has long given it a strategic value, recognised certainly since Viking times when *Orkneyinga Saga* records that Earl Paul had beacons built on Fair Isle and North Ronaldsay and several other islands so that each could be seen from the other and thus give warning of enemy approach from the north. 'There was a man called Dagfinn Hlodvisson, a stout-hearted farmer on Fair Isle, charged with the task of guarding the beacon there and setting fire to it if the enemy fleet were to be seen approaching from Shetland.' In the early 19th century a semaphore was set up for a similar purpose: its base and one of its wooden arms still stand on Malcolm's Head (HZ 195707) not far from the modern coastguard's lookout. The semaphore consisted of a tall pole with moveable arms, and it was used to signal shipping movements to warships patrolling between Orkney and Shetland.

When Sir Walter Scott visited Fair Isle with Commissioners of the Northern Lights in 1814, he dined with the Master of Fair Isle at the Haa, then the largest house on the island though very modest by Shetland and Orkney standards. It stands above the South Harbour, which was the normal landing-place, and it is a simple rectangular two-storey building with crowstepped gables (HZ 203700). It was probably built in the 18th century by an Orcadian family living on Westray, the Stewarts of Brough, who bought Fair Isle from its previous Shetland owner in 1766, for their factor, and its structure has been little altered (including roof-timbers made from wrecked ships). A 19th century corn-drying kiln may be seen at Taft, and there are the ruins of nine horizontal water-mills on the Gilsetter Burn which, like so many Shetland mills, were abandoned during the First World War. Also of interest are the stone-lined boat-nausts to be seen at the shore of Kirkigeo and South Harbour, which sheltered the long narrow Fair Isle yoles over the winter.

The modern distribution of settlement is markedly confined to the southern half of the island, the northern uplands being used for common grazing, and it would seem that this economic division has a very long history. The ancient Feelie Dyke or turf dyke is still a conspicuous boundary, its route across the middle of the island underlined by the accompanying modern drystone dyke.

Fair Isle, south lighthouse and semaphore mast

Fair Isle, The Landberg

Recent fieldwork has identified a number of prehistoric settlements in the form of hut-circles, field-systems and boundary dykes, but at present the earliest evidence of human activity is a bronze-age burial cairn near Fuiniquoy Hill (HZ 212718), in the centre of which was found a cremated burial in a pottery Cinerary Urn, dating to some time before 1000 BC. Fair Isle was quite densely inhabited during the first millennium BC, for there are a number of burnt mounds (see section 10) including, at Vaasetter (HZ 207715), one of the largest such mounds of burnt stone in the Northern Isles, as well as hut-circles and field-systems. Nor did the island escape the social unrest and aggression of the later iron age, for the remains of a fort may be seen at The Landberg, a narrow promontory between South Haven and Mavers Geo (HZ 222722) beside two excellent natural

harbours. A series of three earthen ramparts with shallow ditches between them guard the gently sloping landward approach, while a natural rift caused by a rock fault across the narrow neck of the promontory provided a ready-made obstacle; at the top of the steep slope beyond stands the main rampart, with a few of the large stones of its outer face still visible.

Fair Isle may be reached by the twice-weekly mailboat in summer from Grutness, near Sumburgh in Shetland, or by Loganair from Tingwall, Lerwick. The George Waterston Memorial Centre includes a collection of traditional farm implements and domestic tools as well as displays about the island's natural history.

3

HARBOURS AND TOWNS

Trading relations between the Northern Isles and Norway developed during the Viking Age but became more formal with the activities of Hanseatic merchants from the early 15th century onwards, increasing with the relative economic freedom that came with the pledging of the islands in 1468 and 1469. Shetland in particular became heavily involved in Hanseatic trade in the later 15th and 16th centuries, although it was apparently never as strictly regimented as the Hanseatic ideal demanded: Shetland goods ought to have been traded only through the market in Bergen, but in reality there was unofficial trade direct with individual Hanseatic merchants, despite constant complaints from Bergen. From the trading records kept by Hanseatic towns, as well as from merchants' tombstones in Shetland (see no. 46), we know the origins of the merchants who came to Shetland: they came from Bremen, Hamburg, Lübeck, Danzig and other Baltic ports, setting out in the spring and returning in the late summer. The main attraction of Shetland in trading terms was fish, but the merchants also bought butter, wool and feathers, and with them for sale to the islanders they brought beer, meal, salt and cloth. To begin with in the 15th century the fish were split open and dried on the beach, but by the 17th century Shetland herring was being preserved in salt in barrels—the forerunner of the herring boom of the late 19th and 20th centuries.

The merchants needed trading-booths and storehouses, which they built or rented, and an outstanding example of such a booth, together with its harbour, may be seen at Symbister on Whalsay (no. 9).

The Hanseatic trade came to an end in the early years of the 18th century with increasing pressure to pay customs, a decisive drawback imposed by the Act of Union in 1707. An important new market for dried fish from Shetland was established in the 1730s in Spain, and this was to remain a major source of income until the late 19th century. Remains of fishing stations with their drying beaches may be seen in several places, including the Böd of Grimista in Lerwick (no. 8); the pier at Ollaberry on the northern tip of Shetland mainland (HU 365805) retains a fine 19th century post-crane. Although it had its good times and bad times, fishing was a more vital part of Shetland economy from the 15th century into the 20th century than it was for Orkney: there fishing remained a part-time occupation and, even when herring fishing developed in the late 19th century, most of the big fishing boats involved were not local to Orkney. The major herring fishing stations were on Stronsay and at Stromness, but there was nothing to compare with the scenes of intensive activity at Lerwick, with Bressay Sound full of ships and beaches lined with women gutting the fish.

Lerwick lodberries (no. 12)

33

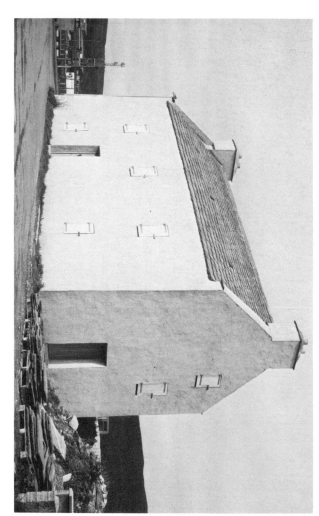

Böd of Gremista, Lerwick (no. 8)

8 Böd of Gremista, Lerwick, Shetland
18th century AD.

HU 464431. Take the A 970 N out of Lerwick; at the point where the road turns inland, take the minor road to the right which leads N along the shore to Point of Scattland, turning right again almost immediately to the shore itself and to the Böd.

The Böd of Gremista is most famous as the birthplace in 1792 of Arthur Anderson, co-founder of the P and O Line, MP for Shetland and initiator of the Shetland Fisheries Company aimed at improving the lot of Shetland fishermen. It is a large rectangular building of uncertain date facing the shore, two storeys high with an attic, with white harled walls and a roof of Caithness slates. Restoration has included external wooden storm shutters to the windows. It was at one time the office and stores for a company who dried fish on the shore.

9 Pier House, Symbister, Whalsay
17th century AD.

HU 539623. Take the car ferry from Laxa Voe to Symbister harbour on Whalsay, follow the harbour road round to the NE side of the harbour.

The excellence of Symbister harbour may be judged from the series of piers and buildings that represent constant activity from the 17th century onwards—and it was undoubtedly used even before then, though no structural traces survive. At one time the entire harbour was lined with a sea-wall, but this has suffered erosion by the sea; there are two modern piers and a rock-built breakwater on the south-west side of the harbour, with a small inner harbour and a large warehouse with an arched entrance. The earliest buildings lie on the eastern side of the large harbour.

The Pier House is an attractive small building set at the end of its own jetty to one side of its own small stone-lined harbour. It has recently been beautifully restored as a visitor centre—to the extent that even the slates on the new roof are held by traditional wooden pegs. Set gable-end to the sea, this two-storey building has a separate entrance to each floor in the landward gable, the upper storey being reached by an external stair. The upper storey served as living quarters with a fireplace, as well as having access to the windlass mechanism set in its external projecting bay. Goods were hoisted from the boat below into the ground-floor storeroom, through double wooden doors that could be closed with a bar. The walls are almost a metre thick, built of rubble with good freestone dressings to the windows and upper doorway; the upper part of the gables built of neat stone blocks are of later date.

Whalsay Sound and the harbour are twice mentioned in 16th century records in the Bremen State Archives, but the surviving booth is probably of 18th century date. Old maps show that the road

Pier House, Whalsay (no. 9)
Pier House, Whalsay (no. 9)

leading down the hill to the booth was once known as the Bremenstrasse. But it is also likely that the larger and much altered house facing on to the small harbour was originally a Hanseatic booth as well. Another early storehouse stands on the shore a little to the south, though converted to modern use with new doors on the landward side and a corrugated iron roof. The original arched entrance may be seen in the seaward gable, and the narrow slits in the long walls (many now filled by small stones) were designed to provide the maximum ventilation and minimum light required to store such goods as dried fish.

Plan showing the early development of Kirkwall (no. 10)

10 Kirkwall, Orkney
HY 4511.

The modern town of Kirkwall has a long and fascinating history of development that is largely masked by its present appearance. The practical orientation of the town today gives the impression of development on either side of a main street running down to the harbour on Kirkwall Bay, though the bleak and largely modern waterfront should give the game away. The clue lies in the Peerie Sea, now a small loch separated from the the bay by a sandspit known as the Aire but once very much bigger and a natural harbour at the head of the bay: the line running approximately north-south and formed by Albert Street, Broad Street and Victoria Street marks the old shoreline in the medieval period. The process of reclamation of land to the west of that line began very slowly from the 13th century onwards until by

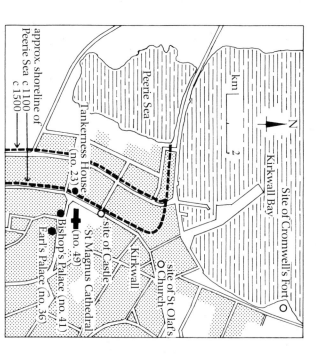

approx. shoreline of
Peerie Sea c 1100
c 1500

1861 the line of Junction Road marked the contemporary shoreline after 100 m of land had been reclaimed (partly by dumping of rubble and earth and partly by natural build-up of shingle). Today the Peerie Sea has shrunk still smaller and its shore lies some 250 m from the medieval water-front.

To judge by references in *Orkneyinga Saga* and artefacts found in recent excavations, there was Viking-age settlement at Kirkwall (ON *Kirkjuvágr*: church bay) perhaps even before the earliest church was built in the 11th century, but nothing is known of its buildings and it was certainly no urban centre to rival the Norse trading towns of Dublin or York, despite the political importance of the Orkney earldom. Little of the church of St Olaf survives, apart from an attractive carved stone doorway with a round arch, apparently not in its original position but close by, in St Olaf's Wynd off Bridge Street. An 11th century hogback tombstone was recovered in the early 1970s from the site of St Olaf's churchyard and is now in Tankerness House Museum. The oldest part of Kirkwall, about which least is known, was around and to the north of this church.

Once the building of St Magnus Cathedral was under way from 1137, a second focus of settlement grew up to the south of the first, above the shore of the Peerie Sea. When James III created the royal burgh of Kirkwall in 1486, his charter refers specifically to the two areas of Burgh and Laverock, the former the old town and the latter the diocesan domain around the cathedral. The oldest domestic buildings surviving are parts of the Bishop's Palace (no. 41), begun in the 12th century, and Tankerness House (no. 23), probably of early 16th century date. Nothing remains of the castle built in the 14th century by the Sinclairs apart from an armorial panel on a later building in Castle Street; it stood on the site of the modern junction between Castle Street, Albert Street and Broad Street, and increasing evidence for the topography of the medieval town suggests that the castle projected out from the shore and was lapped by the sea. It was destroyed in 1615 and its ruins finally demolished in 1865.

Another 16th century building is the Old Grammar School at no. 36 Broad Street, and there is 16th century fabric incorporated into other later buildings, especially in Palace Street and Bishop Reid's house in Victoria Street (now nos 48, 50 and 52). It is worth exploring the older streets, for there are many interesting architectural legacies to be seen: Broad Street and Victoria Street contain many 17th century houses and carved stone fragments. The Girnell (no. 22 Harbour Street), along with the adjacent girnell-keeper's house, was built in the early 17th century as the storehouse for the grain paid as rent in kind to the Earl—the grain was stored in wooden chests or girnells. It is a two-storey building with a basement and two external forestairs. Kirkwall's mercat cross was set up in 1621, originally at the west end of the Strynd but it was moved in the 18th century to the green in front of the cathedral (the original cross is now inside the cathedral and a replica stands outside).

The most spectacular 17th century building is the Earl's Palace (no. 36), architecturally at least a fitting neighbour to the cathedral even though the means by which it was built, forced labour, must initially have made it a hated symbol of oppression.

Adjacent to the Earl's Palace is the Sheriff Court Building, built 1876-7 to a design by the Edinburgh architect David Bryce; by this time Bryce had already successfully completed two major projects in Orkney (Balfour Castle, no. 15, and Trumland House, no. 14), and his confidence was such that initially he had proposed restoring the Earl's Palace itself. The Police Commissioners preferred to build anew—for which we should perhaps be thankful—and the present, fairly austere Sheriff Court Building stands alongside and in

St Olaf's Church doorway, Kirkwall (no. 10)

The Girnell, Kirkwall (no. 10)

Sheriff Court Building, Kirkwall (no. 10)

pleasant contrast to the earlier ornate residence of the earls of Orkney.

Notable among other 19th century buildings are the group of artisans' dwellings built early that century at no. 22 St Catherine's Place (two-storeyed with crowstepped gables) and the Town Hall, built by the Kirkwall architect, T S Peace, between 1884-7 at the corner of Broad Street and St Magnus Lane, with a pilastered entrance in Scots Renaissance style surmounted by the burgh coat-of-arms and statues.

Despite both its potential as a harbour and its status as the power-centre of Orkney, Kirkwall failed to become a thriving port to equal Stromness or Lerwick (unlike the latter, Kirkwall's location could not make it vital to northbound shipping). This is not to deny that trading patterns existed or to imply that Kirkwall was a backwater—finds of pottery and clay pipes from buried occupation levels demonstrate that merchants were trading with east coast Scottish ports and possibly with the Low Countries during the 13th to 17th centuries—but it is significant that there were no substantial harbour facilities until the early 19th century.

11 Stromness, Orkney

HY 2508.

Despite the excellent shelter of Hamnavoe, Stromness, like Lerwick, was slow to develop into a major harbour—in fact it became a burgh only as recently as 1817. Most of the older buildings along its waterfront reflect development in the 18th century, when houses and storehouses were built gable-end to the sea, with their own storehouses and piers furnished with post-cranes for loading and unloading the boats. These buildings may be seen along Victoria Street, Graham Place and Dundas Street, a particularly fine example restored as the Pier Arts Centre. The paved thoroughfare with its archaic air is in fact no earlier than the mid 19th century, and its crooked alignment

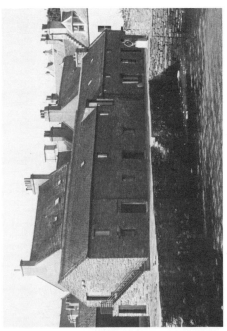

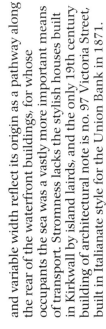

Stromness harbour (no. 11)

Pier Arts Centre, Stromness (no. 11)

and variable width reflect its origin as a pathway along the rear of the waterfront buildings, for whose occupants the sea was a vastly more important means of transport. Stromness lacks the stylish houses built in Kirkwall by island lairds, and the only 19th century building of architectural note is no. 97 Victoria Street, built in Italianate style for the Union Bank in 1871.

The growth of Stromness in the 18th century was closely connected with the arctic whaling industry and in particular with the Hudson's Bay Company, whose ships not only recruited Orcadian crew but also bought their last fresh provisions before the long haul across the Atlantic–Login's Well (South End) filled the water-barrels of many famous ships, and the cannon on the seaward side of Ness Road, reputedly taken from an American privateer in 1813, was fired to signal the arrival of Hudson's Bay Company ships.

Alfred Street, Stromness (no. 11) by Erskine Beveridge, 1894

12 Lerwick
HU 4741.

Bressay Sound is a kilometre wide stretch of water between the island of Bressay and the curve of the peninsula now occupied by the town of Lerwick, and it has provided ideal shelter for large numbers of ships, especially in the great days of the haaf and herring fishing. Yet Lerwick is quite a young town, founded only in the 17th century. Its bay was named by the Norsemen, *leir vik* or mud bay, but this part of Shetland was unattractive for early settlement, the land being relatively infertile, and it was Scalloway on the west coast that first developed as the capital for the islands. By the 17th century, Bressay Sound had been adopted by Dutch fishermen as a base, and a seasonal trading post developed at Lerwick specifically to do business with the Hollanders. But it was the war between Britain and Holland in the mid 17th century that led to the permanent foundation of the town, with the construction of Fort Charlotte (no. 4) to guard the anchorage in Bressay Sound for British warships.

Apart from the fort, the oldest buildings surviving in recognisable form in Lerwick belong to the 18th century and are to be found along the seaward side of Commercial Street, the dwelling-houses fronting on to the street and the lodberries behind, private wharves built projecting into the sea with storehouses and facilities for landing goods. No. 10 is a fine example, recently restored, of a merchant's house fronting on to the street: two-stories high with an attic, the house is rubble-built with freestone dressings to the windows and front door, crowstepped gables and a

The Lodberry, Lerwick (no. 12)

Town Hall, Lerwick (no. 12)

slated roof, and behind it there is a lodberry. The buildings now known simply as The Lodberry consist of a single-storey house which acted as a shop fronting on to the street, with a two-storey house attached, gable-end on, to the rear, and a lodberry with its loading door and ventilated storehouse above. The Lerwick waterfront, like that at Stromness, has a very distinctive and attractive appearance, for the projecting lodberries are all slightly different in size and design, as their form, and latterly function, has developed over the last two centuries. The Queen's Hotel has converted its two lodberries, probably of early 19th century date, to accommodation wings. The old town tolbooth at no. 32 Commercial Street was built in the late 1760s on the site of an earlier tolbooth—the scrolled skewputts on its gables are very similar to

those on Busta House near Brae (no. 18). Another recently restored 18th century merchant's house is the Böd of Grimista (no. 8), built beside a fish-drying beach at the very north end of modern Lerwick.

A number of fine public buildings were erected in the late 19th century, including St Magnus Episcopal Church (1864) with its crenellated tower (1891), and the attractively modest Sheriff Court (1875), designed by David Rhind of Edinburgh. Far more ornate is the imposing Town Hall (1883), designed in Scottish Baronial style by Alexander Ross, with its angle-turrets, oriel window over the main entrance and crenellated clock-tower, together with many decorative details including a remarkable series of stained glass windows in the first-floor ballroom.

4

COUNTRY MANSIONS,
TOWN HOUSES AND DOVECOTES

The Northern Isles cannot boast of any architecture on a scale to match the great stately homes of other parts of Scotland, for most of the larger houses are modest both in size and architectural distinction, but in many cases this is amply recompensed by their setting: seascapes that change from calm tranquillity to dramatic turbulence, from clear vistas of distant islands and headlands to the spray-blurred outlines of a land dominated by the sea. The architects responsible for the larger houses made their setting very much part of the overall design, though it is a matter of personal taste whether the elaborate Scottish Baronial style of 19th century country mansions such as Balfour Castle (no. 15) really suit their landscape. The Balfour family of Shapinsay commissioned the great exponent of Scottish Baronial architecture, David Bryce of Edinburgh, to design not only the family seat on Shapinsay between 1846 and 1850 but also their house near Kirkwall in 1850, although the latter, Berstane House (HY 468103), is a far more modest house in the Picturesque Villa style. Through Balfour influence on Orkney County Council, Bryce was also commissioned to design Kirkwall Sheriff Court Building in 1872, in which year he designed Trumland House on Rousay (no. 14) for another powerful Orcadian family, this time adopting a Scottish Jacobean theme.

Trumland House was unusual in being an entirely new building, for most 19th and 20th century designs

involved enlarging an existing house. Indeed most rural houses, great or small, surviving today represent the culmination of structural additions or modifications over the years, and it can often prove difficult to identify the original house: Busta House (no. 18) seems to have grown almost imperceptibly, the result is so harmonious. It was this sense of blending in with and belonging to the old order that WR Lethaby achieved at Melsetter on Hoy (no. 13) in 1898, where he extended and amalgamated an earlier house and outbuildings; Lethaby was part of the Arts and Crafts movement of the late 19th and early 20th century, in which hand-crafted products and a reverence for local building traditions were essential, and Melsetter House is considered to be one of the most radical examples of these ideals—and the best of Lethaby's own small body of work. It is said that he was so moved by the original Melsetter and its landscape that he tore up the plans that he had designed in London and began afresh. The result was described by May Morris, daughter of William Morris, as 'a sort of fairy palace on the edge of the great northern seas'. His client, an industrialist from Birmingham named Thomas Middlemore, also owned the islands of Rysa and Fara, and Lethaby built another smaller house for him at Rysa Lodge (ND 306962) on the east coast of Hoy, overlooking Rysa Bay and the two small islands beyond. Completed in 1902, Rysa Lodge was again an extension of an earlier building, this time adopting a single-storey croft house.

Skaill House, Orkney (no. 19)

It may well have been Lethaby's interest in old buildings that prompted Thomas Middlemore to have the old monastery on Eynhallow cleared of debris; Middlemore owned the island of Eynhallow, and, when the church and its outbuildings were disentangled from later structures in 1897, he and his architect friend Lethaby were present to examine the buildings (no. 52). The party stayed in a timber-built lodge, painted white, which unfortunately no longer exists.

A greater loss is another timber building that burned down in the early years of the 20th century: the Clousta Hotel in Shetland. This was a custom-built fisherman's hotel, designed by the famous Scottish architect, R S Lorimer, in 1894, and it was set in some of Scotland's most beautiful scenery, amongst the lochs and hills and voe-indented coastline of north-west mainland.

Contemporary with Lethaby's work on Hoy but in complete contrast is the house built on Vaila in Shetland between 1895 and 1900 by a Yorkshire industrialist, Herbert Anderton (no. 17). Little attempt was made to incorporate the existing late 17th century house other than as an appendage, and the new Vaila Hall was built in Scottish Jacobean style with castellated parapets, crowstepped gables and, as a local note, turret-supports with alternate corbels echoing those at Scalloway and Muness castles (nos 37 and 38).

In the earlier 19th century an elegant Georgian mansion was created at Symbister on Whalsay (no. 16), and a year earlier, in 1829, a townhouse in Kirkwall was extended and modified into a fine Georgian residence with a pilastered entrance: Custom House, no. 33 Albert Street. Aside from such buildings as these, landowners continued to use and to modify the older houses dating from the 16th and 17th centuries. The typical laird's house in Shetland is a plain rectangular building of two storeys and an attic

(eg no. 22), but there seems to have been more variety in Orkney and in particular a liking for the courtyard plan, derived from the design of the grand palaces such as the Earl's Palace at Birsay (no. 39). This led to some very beautiful houses, which have a special affinity with their landscape, such as Langskaill House on Gairsay (no. 20), and which could blend equally well with the Kirkwall townscape in the case of Tankerness House (no. 23).

The Palace at Kirkwall (no. 36), the Palace at Birsay which his father built (no. 39) and the castle at Scalloway (no. 37) take pride of place among the surviving properties of Earl Patrick, but there are also remains of a 'house and fortalice' that he owned on Sumburgh Head (no. 24). From contemporary documentary sources, it seems that Sumburgh (now known as Jarlshof) was used as an administrative centre in Earl Robert's time, for it housed the local law-court when necessary, and it is unlikely that it was in any real sense the Earl's residence for either Earl. There is a marked contrast between the modest building of Sumburgh and the lavish Orkney palaces.

Dovecotes

In medieval and later times, most landowners of any substance included a dovecote on their estates. Keeping pigeons for the table provided variety of diet and, in the winter, a much-needed extra source of food, and the fact that the pigeons fed indiscriminately off crops in the vicinity was a disadvantage only to poorer neighbours. There is considerable variety of form amongst dovecotes in Orkney and Shetland, from the beehive shape of that at Hall of Rendall (no. 25), perhaps the earliest surviving example dating from the 16th or 17th century, to the square type seen at Sand Lodge, Shetland (HU 436247) and the cylindrical form at Busta (no. 18), as well as the more common rectangular dovecotes. Several can still be appreciated within the context of the house and estate to which they belonged, eg nos 13, 16, 18, 19.

In all cases, the dovecote has a single chamber lined internally with small nesting-boxes (usually about 500), which is entered through a ground-level door and by pigeons through small openings in the roof or high up in the walls; there are often projecting string-courses in the external masonry, designed to prevent rats and other predators from climbing the walls. Circular dovecotes had domed or conical roofs, while the rectangular type is often known as the lectern owing to its flat sloping roof (usually facing south) and projecting, often crowstepped, gables. For the most part, the roofs no longer survive, but, apart from those mentioned below, good examples of 17th and 18th century dovecotes may be seen at Woodwick, Orkney (HY 390240), Warsetter, Sanday, Orkney (HY 630377) and Holland, Papa Westray, Orkney (HY 488515).

Decorative arch and gun-loops.
Langskaill House, Gairsay (no. 20)

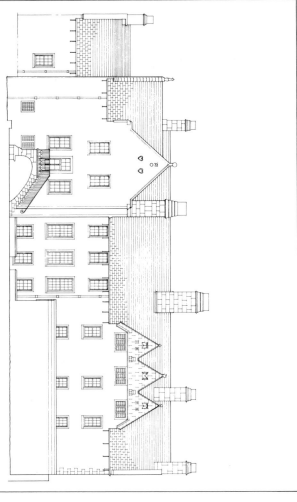

East elevation of Melsetter House, Hoy, by J Brandon-Jones (no. 13)

13 Melsetter House, Hoy, Orkney

AD 1898.
ND 270893. At the S end of Hoy overlooking North Bay and Longhope.

Melsetter House and Rysa Lodge on Hoy are William R Lethaby's sole works in Scotland and among his very few creations anywhere, for he was a theoretician rather than a practical architect. At Melsetter he was able to incorporate both the original house, an L-shaped two-storey building of 1738, and some outbuildings into a mellow and intimate country house with paved courtyard and walled gardens. Moreover he was able to inject into the overall design the magic quality and fundamental symbolism of his architectural ideal; the symbolism appears in tangible form as a star and moon carved from stone and two small heart-shaped windows with stone mouldings on the south gable of the east front of the house. The magic quality was certainly felt by May Morris, daughter of William Morris, who had helped to found the so-called Arts and Crafts movement in architecture and interior design: she wrote of Melsetter that it seemed 'the embodiment of some of those fairy palaces of which my father wrote with great charm and dignity. But, for all its fitness and dignity, it was a place full of homeliness and the spirit of welcome, a very loveable place'. May Morris was a friend of Theodosia Middlemore, wife of the industrialist who had bought the Melsetter estate and herself an embroideress and weaver. Both Middlemores were appropriate patrons for an idealist like Lethaby and with Melsetter they had provided him with a perfect stimulus. He adopted local traditions of building, harling the exterior walls, using local sandstone for dressings and Caithness flags for the roof and featuring crowstepped gables, but adding his own distinctive mark, particularly on the great fireplace in the entrance hall where a finely moulded surround to the fire itself is surmounted by five stone corbels designed as rests for candles which would throw into dramatic relief a row of seven coats of arms carved into the stonework above. The visual effect was enhanced by tapestries and silken wall-hangings, some of which were made in the Morris workshop.

The south wing of Lethaby's house is the original 18th century house with its vaulted morning room, and a contemporary square dovecote was incorporated into the south-west corner of the walled garden, balanced by a tea-house on the south-east corner.

14 Trumland House, Rousay, Orkney

AD 1872-3.

HY 428277. Close to the SE coast of Rousay, 1 km from Brinyan pier.

An unusually sheltered spot was chosen for this house, a small valley through which a burn runs down to the sea and where it has been possible to coax woodland to grow. Previously the family seat of the Traill family of Rousay was the 18th century Westness House (HY 383290), but, after his marriage, Lt Gen Frederick W Traill Burroughs decided to commission the celebrated architect, David Bruce, to design a more imposing residence. The result was a mansion in the Scottish Jacobean style, three storeys high with an attic—the first owner's initials and the date 1873 are carved on a panel above the rear door.

Scottish Baronial style, with a square castellated tower rising above the main entrance, further embellished with a corner turret, with huge bay windows to the public rooms, square turrets with pyramidal roofs, round turrets with conical roofs, crowstepped gables and a glorious conservatory almost as large as the drawingroom. The main stair remained in the central, older portion of the now Z-shaped house, but, typical of such Bryce designs, the public rooms are served by an immensely long and broad corridor into which the new main entrance opens.

The extraordinary gateway over the path leading to the kitchen-garden is built of sculptured stones found in the vicinity of St Mary's church and the Wirk (HY 373302; see Rousay excursion). They are high quality architectural fragments, carved of red sandstone, some of 13th century date and some of 16th century date, and it is thought that the 13th century pieces may have been 'spares' from St Magnus Cathedral. More architectural fragments are built into the east end of the later St Mary's church, and others were found in the debris of the monastery on Eynhallow (no. 52).

15 Balfour Castle, Shapinsay, Orkney

Mid 19th century AD.

HY 474164. About 1.5 km W of the pier; ferry from Kirkwall.

Between 1846 and 1850, David Bryce designed his first large commission for David Balfour of Shapinsay: his remit to enlarge the existing family house overlooking the sheltered bay of Elwick. It was an invitation to design on a lavish scale, and accordingly Bryce created an outstanding example of a country mansion in

Bryce may also have designed the imposing entrance into the grounds of the Castle, which consists of an archway with a mock portcullis and flanking lodges, the whole gateway capped by a corbelled parapet. The grounds were laid out by Craigie Halkett Inglis of Cramond, Edinburgh, and they include an elaborate 17th century gateway. This belonged to an earlier house that was burned down by Hanoverian soldiers in 1746 and replaced by the L-shaped building incorporated into Bryce's grand design. It suits well the Baronial style of the later mansion. A moulded archway is flanked by columns and topped with a pediment bearing an armorial panel, the whole composition richly decorated: mermaids holding harps, men and animals playing musical instruments, and, flanking the armorial panel, unicorns and caryatid figures in 17th century costume. The coats of arms and initials are those of Arthur Buchanan and Margaret Buxton and are identical to those at Carrick House on Eday (no. 21), though the date here is 1674, twelve years later than the Carrick panel.

Another legacy from the 17th century is Dishan Tower, a circular dovecote now somewhat oddly situated on the rocky foreshore, which was restored equally oddly in the 19th century as a 'douche-house', taking advantage of its proximity to the sea to provide a salt-water shower. This too is embellished with a corbelled and crenellated parapet and a crowstepped cap-house.

Balfour Castle, Shapinsay (no. 15)

Shapinsay was the scene of feverish building activity in the early-mid 19th century, for as well as the castle and its grounds Colonel Balfour also 'improved' the island as a whole, creating a planned village, now known as Balfour Village, on Elwick Bay for the workers on his estate.

16 Symbister House, Whalsay, Shetland
AD 1830.
HU 542621. About 1 km SE of the pier; ferry from Laxa Voe.

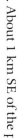

Set conspicuously above the harbour, this is the most outstanding Georgian mansion in the Northern Isles, with its imposing facade and symmetrical layout of offices behind. It was built by Robert Bruce of Symbister in 1830, replacing an earlier house, and since 1940 it has been converted into a school. The house consists of two storeys with a basement and an attic, and the impressive entrance with its columned portico is reached by a stair—the upper of the two string-courses is aligned with the top of the portico. On the west side of the house, above a gateway in a screen-wall leading to a rear entrance, there is a fine armorial panel in excellent condition, which must have come from the earlier house; it bears the date 1750. The formal ranges behind the house include stables and coach-houses and central belfry and dovecote towers—the latter decorated with an extraordinary quatrefoil recess filled with stone balls.

17 Vaila Hall, Vaila, Shetland
AD 1696 and 1895-1900.
HU 226468. On the N side of the island; access by boat and by prior arrangement with R H Anderton, Spurries House, Walls.

The small island of Vaila lies just off the coast of south-west mainland Shetland, and a beautiful view of the island and the house may be enjoyed by climbing the hill above Burrastow on the adjacent mainland across Wester Sound. Vaila itself rises to a height of 80 m OD on the south side where there are dramatic cliffs and stacks, and on the lower slopes there are a number of burnt mounds (see section 10) which testify to the attraction of the island in prehistoric times. In recent centuries settlement has been concentrated in the northern part overlooking Vaila Sound and mainland.

Muckle Flugga lighthouse, Unst

Fair Isle, west coast with the south lighthouse

Symbister House, Whalsay,
(no. 16)

Pier House, Whalsay (no. 9)

The original Vaila House was a plain rectangular building with crowstepped gables, consisting of two storeys and a garret, and this is now the south side of the later house. The original entrance, which opens directly into the Great Hall, still retains its moulded stone surround and battered armorial panel above: this depicts the arms and motto of the Mitchell family and the date 1696. The old doorway well suits the Great Hall with its Jacobean oak furniture and baronial air.

In 1893 the island was sold to Herbert Anderton, a Yorkshire mill owner with interests in Shetland wool; he commissioned a large new house in Scottish Jacobean style as well as building a house for his farm-manager, a boat-house with a studio above at Ham,

and restoring the old tower west of the big house as an observatory. The new Vaila Hall was built in the final years of the 19th century in a style popular since the middle years of that century, though less elaborate than many; it is a solid two-storey building, facing west, with crowstepped gables to match the old house and embellished with corbelled wall-heads, castellated parapets, a circular corner-tower and castellated turrets supported on decorative corbelling.

Burrastow House on the adjacent mainland (HU 223478, now a hotel) illustrates in its main block the type of house to which the original Vaila belonged. On the way to Burrastow from Walls, there are two clack mills (see section 5) close to the road at HU 215485).

Burrastow House, Walls, Shetland

18 Busta House, Shetland

*16th and 18th centuries AD.
HU 345667. On the A 970 between Voe and Hillswick, take the minor road about 1 km beyond Brae which leads S along Busta Voe; signposted (now a hotel).*

The immediate surroundings of Busta House are sufficiently sheltered to have allowed trees to mature around it and yet it enjoys a magnificent view across Busta Voe and beyond. An early 19th century visitor so admired the garden with its mountain ashes, plane trees and elders after a long and bleak journey that he wrote: 'nothing can give greater cheer to the fatigued vision, when so long satiated with the superfluous waste of bare and tenantless scatholds'. At that time Shetland possessed very few surfaced roads, but Busta had its own paved road stretching out some 1.5 km into that bare landscape. The composite house of today is the result of several phases of building, and the overall effect is very pleasing; from the house itself to its terraced grounds embellished by pairs of carved stone gargoyles—acquired many years ago during restoration of the House of Commons in London!

The original 16th century house was a modest two-storey rectangular building with crowstepped gables, which was bought by the Gifford family in the 17th century. A new three-storey mansion was added in 1714, at the time of the marriage of Thomas Gifford and Elizabeth Mitchell, and the carved stone armorial panel over the entrance is the same as that over the entrance of their burial aisle at Voe (no. 44) together a phase of building that provided for the future both in life and in death. The new house was added somewhat asymmetrically to the north gable of the old, so that the new main entrance opens on to the angle between the two. The arched doorway has a moulded stone surround, as do some internal doorways and fireplaces, and the gables are finished with spiral skewputts. The entrance opens into a stair-wing

19 Skaill House, Sandwick, Orkney

17th century AD and later.
HY 234186. From Stromness N on the A 967, take the B 9056 to Sandwick.

As it stands today, Skaill House is rather closer to the sea than it was two hundred years ago: a map drawn in 1772 shows the house exactly half-way between the Bay of Skaill and the freshwater loch of Skaill, quite close to the burn running from the loch into the sea. The size and shape of the bay has changed over the centuries—amongst other things leading to the discovery of the prehistoric settlement of Skara Brae (no. 72)—and it was clearly proximity to a source of freshwater that determined the location of the house. The same map shows the house as a single block with outbuildings, and the oldest part of the house surviving today is indeed a rectangular block, with the original entrance facing southwards and inland rather than towards the sea, and this, the old Hall of Skaill, is likely to date from the early 17th century or earlier.

Since then there have been considerable additions and alterations: the old Hall and its outbuildings linked by a screen-wall to create a typical courtyard complex as at Langskaill on Gairsay (no. 20), and then another block parallel to the Hall and linked by a short central block to form an H-shaped mansion on the south side of the courtyard. The gable-ends of the two wings of the mansions were later linked by short screen-walls, so that the west side of the entire complex is now one long facade consisting of three gable-walls and two screen-walls with gateways. Various pieces of stone-carving have been re-used over the two gateways and on the modern porch on the east side of the house, including an armorial panel from Bishop Graham's ruined Breckness House near Stromness, an early 17th century house owned then by the same Graham family that owned Skaill. There is also a rectangular 18th century dovecote beside the house.

projecting from the main block, and the stair itself has a fine stone balustrade.

Below the house is a small stone-built harbour, and, on the headland to the north-east (HU 347669), there is a circular dovecote, roofless but otherwise intact, which is likely to date from the early 18th century.

Dovecote, Busta House, Shetland (no. 18)

Skaill House, Orkney (no. 19)

20 Langskaill House, Gairsay, Orkney
17th century AD.
HY 434219. Close to the SW shore of the island.

Langskaill House, Gairsay (no. 20)

Langskaill House, Gairsay: courtyard (no. 20)

Gairsay is a very attractive small island with a sheltered anchorage in Millburn Bay, and it is not surprising that it was part of a prestigious Norse family estate in the 12th century, conveniently situated as it is astride one of the approaches to the bays of Firth and

Kirkwall. *Orkneyinga Saga* tells of the exploits of the Viking Svein Asleifarson who farmed on Gairsay, raided in the Hebrides and Ireland and owned another estate at Duncansby in Caithness, and tradition would locate the remains of his great hall beneath the present Langskaill House.

The house was built soon after 1653 for Sir William Craigie and his wife, Margaret Honyman, whose initials are carved on a lintel over the entrance to the east range of the house. The original design consisted of three such ranges round a courtyard, with a screen-wall across the fourth side, but the north range has been demolished, the west range is derelict and only the east range, restored in about 1900, remains habitable. This is now a single-storey building with an attic, but the south end at least must at one time have been a storey higher, matching the west range, so as to allow access to the parapet along the screen-wall. Although the building was much altered in the early 20th century, two very fine fireplaces survive on the attic floor, with moulded and carved stone jambs and lintels.

The south front gives a marvellous impression of the fortified and yet elegant family house. The screen-wall with its central gateway is flanked to either side by the gable-ends of the east and west ranges, and a moulded stone base-course runs the entire length of the front. The gateway was originally the only means of access to the house, and it is guarded on either side and above by the gun-loops as well as by the parapet—the door itself does not survive, but the slots for the bar that could be drawn across behind the door still exist within the wall on either side. The archway is finely carved with a vine scroll, and on the parapet above there is an elaborate armorial panel crowned with a triangular carved pediment. This was originally even more elaborate, and the rest of the parapet bore a stone balustrade—the whole design must have been very impressive. A similar 17th century gateway survives in the grounds of Balfour Castle on Shapinsay (no. 15).

Langskaill House, Gairsay: gateway (no. 20)

Carrick House, Eday (no. 21)

Above the gateway is an armorial panel with the initials of Arthur Buchanan and his English wife, Marjory Buxton and the date 1662; the same initials and coats of arms appear on the 17th century gateway in the grounds of Balfour Castle on Shapinsay (no. 15). The original owner and builder of the house was John Stewart, Earl of Carrick and brother of Earl Patrick Stewart, who had been granted the entire island in 1632. Since the 18th century, Carrick House has been famous for its part in the capture of the notorious pirate, John Gow, whose exploits inspired Sir Walter Scott's novel 'The Pirate'; in his ship, the 'Revenge', Gow ran aground on the Calf of Eday during an attempt to raid Carrick House in 1725, and he was held prisoner in the house before being sent to London for trial. His ship's bell is still preserved at the house.

21 Carrick House, Eday, Orkney
AD 1633.

HY 566384. Close to the shore at the N end of the island, some 11 km from the main ferry pier at Backaland.

This house is perhaps more notable for its historical associations than for its architecture, but its setting is superb and its view over Calf Sound unrivalled. In its original form in the 17th century, it consisted of a low rectangular house with crowstepped gables and a courtyard enclosed by a stone wall, and the gateway, set on the seaward side because most contemporary visitors would arrive by boat, retains its original moulding and arch, with the date 1633 carved on the keystone of the arch.

Old Hall of Brough, Yell,
before restoration (no. 22)

22 Old Hall (Haa) of Brough, Burravoe, Yell 👤

AD 1672.
HU 520794. Near the shore on a minor road about
0.5 km S of the A 968 at Burravoe.

This 17th century house was built at a point from
which all boats attempting to enter the shelter of
narrow Burra Voe could be monitored—and the
entrance to the courtyard lies on the seaward side, that
being the direction from which most visitors would
come. The modern road cuts through the
courtyard, but the house has been restored and
contains a local history exhibition. The house itself
is a substantial rectangular building with

crowstepped gables from which the remains of the
courtyard walls project on the west side. At some stage
it became necessary to strengthen the long walls of the
house by adding massive buttresses, which do little to
alleviate its stern exterior. The gateway in the south
wall of the courtyard has a rounded arch above which
is an armorial panel within a moulded stone surround:
it bears the date 1672 and the initials R T for the laird,
Robert Tyrie.

In the early 19th century an old trading booth on the
shore of Burra Voe was still owned and operated by
the family living in the Old Haa, selling goods
imported from Scotland.

Tankerness House, Kirkwall (no. 23)

23* Tankerness House, Kirkwall, Orkney
16th-17th century AD.
HY 448108. On Broad Street, almost opposite St Magnus Cathedral; now a museum.

This attractive building is widely regarded as one of the finest early town houses surviving in Scotland, and it has been restored and converted into a museum without losing its essential character. Its present name originated in the 17th century when it became the town residence of the Baikie family of Tankerness, but in the previous century it was the subchantry and archdeanery for St Magnus Cathedral, and the initials of an archdeacon appear on the armorial panel over the entrance gateway: M G F for Master Gilbert Fulzie.

This gateway and the north wing of the house are of 16th century date—the panel over the gateway bears the date 1574, and the initials of Fulzie's wife, Elizabeth Kinnaird. The jambs and arch are heavily moulded and the armorial panel is set into a corbelled parapet. The north wing has two storeys and an attic, and the original spiral stair is housed in a small projecting tower just inside the gateway. Subsequent additions and modifications have created the harmonious courtyard house of today, its almost square courtyard entirely enclosed by buildings. On the west side of the house is a peaceful garden, which is graced by a large architectural fragment from the cathedral.

Jarlshof (no. 24) and Sumburgh
Head lighthouse

24* Jarlshof, Sumburgh Head, Shetland

16th and early 17th centuries.
HU 398095. At the S tip of the Shetland mainland, near Sumburgh Hotel, S from the A 970. HBM (SDD).

The latest in the long sequence of buildings (see no. 55) on this important site is the early 17th century laird's house which overlies part of the prehistoric broch (in fact the broch proved a useful source of building stone for the house). Contemporary Shetlanders knew this house as Sumburgh, and, by the time that Sir Walter Scott re-named it 'Jarlshof' in his novel 'The Pirate', its ruins were virtually buried in wind-blown sand; the passage at the beginning of the novel in which Scott describes the house as he imagined it to have appeared in the late 17th century is fictitious, though probably close to the mark: 'a rude building of rough stone with nothing about it to gratify the eye or to excite the imagination'. It was, nevertheless, a substantial building with two upper storeys, and its accompanying domestic buildings formed the other three sides of a central rectangular courtyard.

The dwelling-house, the south block, was a simple rectangular house, 18 m by 7 m with walls more than a metre thick; the ground-floor was divided into two storerooms, and an external stair (known as a forestair) led from the courtyard into the two rooms on the first floor, each with a fireplace set into the gable wall. There was evidently a garret in the roof space, because a small window survives at that height in the north-west gable. Although the upper floors are incomplete and the building roofless, this is the best preserved block; it was flanked by outhouses of which only the east block survives to a height of almost 4 m, while the building on the north side of the courtyard functioned as the kitchen block. This survives little higher than a metre, but it was originally the house built in Earl Robert's time which was later superseded in 1605 by the house built by Earl Patrick on the south side of the courtyard.

The old house at Sumburgh had a brief and turbulent existence. By the end of the 17th century it was in ruins and a new house, of which no trace now survives, had been built nearby, itself replaced by the 19th century building that is now the Sumburgh Hotel.

25   Hall of Rendall, Dovecote, Orkney

17th century AD.
HY 422207. Near the farmhouse of Hall of Rendall on E coast of mainland, minor road to E from A 966, almost 11 km NE of Finstown.

This attractive beehive dovecote with its four external string-courses is unique in the Northen Isles. The nests for the pigeons are simply irregular gaps left in the rough masonry of the internal wall-face.

Dovecote, Hall of Rendall, Orkney (no. 25), before restoration.

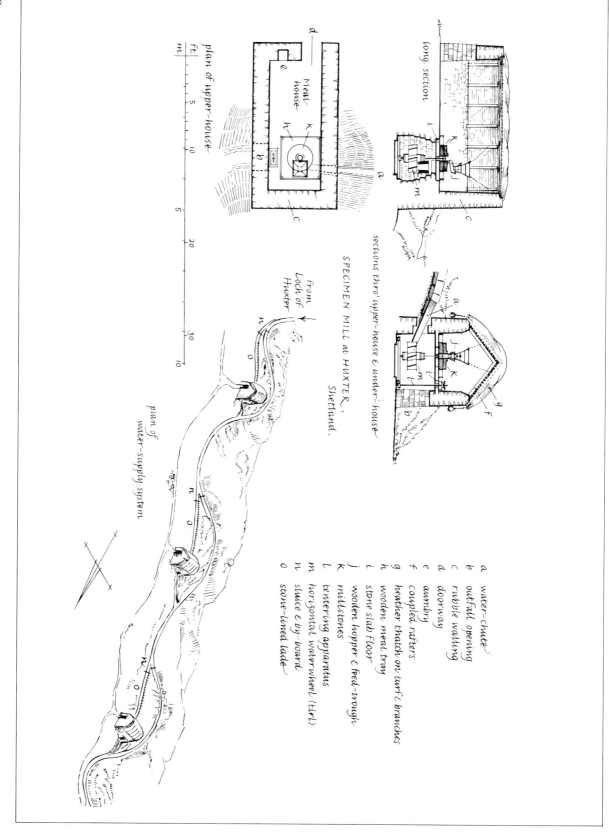

SPECIMEN MILL at HIXTER, Shetland.

plan of upper-house

long section

sections thro' upper-house & under-house

plan of water-supply system

from Loch of Hixter

Meal house

a water-chute
b outfall opening
c rubble walling
d doorway
e aumbry
f coupled rafters
g heather thatch on turf & branches
h wooden meal tray
i stone slab floor
j wooden hopper & feed-trough
k millstones
l tentering apparatus
m horizontal waterwheel (tirl)
n sluice & by-board
o stone-lined lade

Watermills

A very special feature of the Shetland landscape is the small horizontal watermill: several hundred existed at one time, and their ruins are still a familiar sight, though sometimes hidden in steeply-cut water-courses. Visitors to the islands were often struck by the small scale of these mills, including a Scottish minister who in 1845 recorded:

'one of their small, miniature corn-mills lay in our course, and interested our curiosity. The only aperture was so small, that entrance was impossible to one of ordinary dimensions. On looking in, we saw an elderly female knitting a stocking, and occasionally throwing in a handful of bear (bere, barley) into the smallest conceivable millstone, which again was made to revolve by a microscopic horizontal wheel without. How she got in was a mystery only equalled by the problem of how she could get out.'

These mills are small, rectangular drystone buildings, normally windowless and with one door, roofed with flagstones and turf or thatch. They are known as horizontal mills because their water-wheels are set horizontally rather than vertically, and their mechanism is very simple, to the extent that they are really no more than water-powered hand-querns. The two millstones are set at floor-level in the meal-house, the upper stone rotated by the water-wheel or tirl in the under-house below; the tirl consisted of an iron-bound wooden shaft set with inclined wooden blades or feathers, usually eight to twelve in number, and the remains of the tirl can still be seen in many ruined mills, though the fittings of the meal-house above have usually been removed.

Quite a number of these mills were still in use up to and during the First World War, and a few have been kept in working order until recent times by farmers with antiquarian interests—notably one on the Clumlie burn in southern Shetland which is still in working order (HU 407169). Another mill has been restored as

part of the South Voe Croft Museum (no. 26), and the only intact horizontal mill in Orkney is in state care (no. 34). Such mills were never as common in Orkney as in Shetland, for topographical reasons, and Orkney's few good water-courses were early on harnessed by vertical mills serving larger numbers of customers. None of the surviving mills can be dated earlier than the 18th century, but documentary evidence shows that there were mills at least as early as the 15th century, and remains of one of Norse date have been excavated at Orphir; they would normally be demolished and re-built on the same spot, and Boardhouse in Birsay is unusual in retaining a sequence of mills (no. 31). Horizontal mills are sometimes known as Norse mills, but an earlier Irish origin is more likely: the remains of a number of Irish examples have been found in water-logged conditions with preserved timber parts, and tree-ring dating of the wood has shown them to be of Dark Age date between AD 630 and AD 926.

In the Northern Isles, horizontal mills have also been known as click mills or clack mills because of the distinctive sound that they made during operation. The meal was fed into the millstones from a wooden hopper and shoe suspended above, and it was jiggled gently from the shoe or feed trough into the millstones by a clapper; this was usually a stone on the end of a string attached to the shoe which rattled along on the moving millstone, though at Click Mill, Dounby (no. 34), the clapper is a wooden tongue which is struck by a wooden knob on the millstone at every revolution.

Equally interesting at many sites are the external arrangements made to manage the flow of water into the mill, for each had its own stone-lined lade upstream feeding into a timber chute that directed the water on to the water-wheel, and at the head of the lade the sluice had a wooden gate which could be slotted into position to close the sluice and divert the

Plan of Huxter watermills, Shetland (no. 32)

Peckhole windmill, North Ronaldsay, drawing by T S Peace

Windmill base, Holland, Papa Westray

water. These arrangements are particularly well preserved at Huxter (no. 32), as is the dam and first sluice-gate at the feeder loch itself.

Vertical mills could vary in size from one to three storeys, and could be designed either to grind or to thresh grain, though the latter were not introduced into the Northern Isles until the 1820s. The largest vertical mill in Shetland, set in sheltered Weisdale, is Kergord Mill (HU 394530), a substantial two-storey building now unfortunately lacking its wheel.

Windmills

While the small water-driven mill was specially suited to Shetland's steeply rushing burns, windmills were common in Orkney where good water-courses were few but the low-lying windswept landscape ideal for harnessing wind-power. The old windmills went out of use some years ago, but this natural source of power has been harnessed again in recent years, with the erection of several wind turbine power generators, such as that on Burgar Hill, Evie. Orcadian windmills are of the type known as the post mill, the simplest form of windmill known to have existed in Britain from at least as early as the 13th century, though none of the surviving remains in Orkney can be dated earlier than the 18th century. The timber superstructure of the mill revolved upon a conical stone-built 'post', and it is this stone base that survives today. The fine drawing by T S Peace of a windmill in North Ronaldsay enables us to reconstruct the original appearance of such mills: four sails were fitted vertically to the timber mill-house, and a long tail-beam allowed the whole superstructure to be moved round to face the wind. Here the tail-beam is fitted with a wheel to make its movement easier, and the ladder providing access to the mill is attached to the tail-beam as well. The furled canvas sail attached to each wooden-framed sail is visible, along with the simple rigging that allowed the miller to set the sails, and the close relationship between such windmills and the principles of sailing ships is obvious.

Planticrues

Planticrues or planticrubs are a familiar feature of the Shetland landscape, though they were used in Orkney as well. They are small stone-built enclosures, round, square or rectangular and between 3 m and 9 m across, in which young cabbage plants were raised in the shelter of high walls, out of the wind and away from grazing animals. There was no entrance, although some have had gaps for gates knocked out of the wall in recent years: originally access was by projecting stone footholds or by short wooden ladders. Nets could be strung across the smaller planticrues to keep off birds. Very often the walls are built with a basal course of large boulders and smaller stones above, a technique that shows a continuity of tradition from very early times—the same method can be seen in neolithic houses and tombs. Particularly well preserved examples may be seen on Whalsay (see Whalsay excursion), where they have remained in use into recent times, and where their distribution seems to have been related to a freshwater supply rather than to proximity to the owner crofts.

Skeos

At one time, virtually every farm and croft would have had a skeo (Norwegian *skjaa*, drying-house) for storing food supplies and drying fish and meat, but they were going out of use by the early 19th century and few now survive. They were small oblong buildings set in exposed places to catch the wind, their rough stone walls constructed to allow the wind to blow through, and just a narrow doorway. The walls of such a skeo may be seen at the shore below Pinhoulland in Shetland (HU 262498; see no. 76), its interior only about 3 m by 1 m with thick rubble walls.

Occasionally small sheds may be seen in Shetland which use upturned old boats as roofs: there is one beside a field-dyke at Greenland, Walls (HU 227492); such sheds were mostly used to shelter lambs or ducks, though one in Lerwick, beyond the south end of Commercial Street, is now used as a garage.

Ancient Dykes

Field boundaries have been constructed since very early times, and Orkney and Shetland have examples going back to the 3rd and 4th millennia BC. More substantial turf and stone dykes were built as territorial boundaries and as agricultural barriers between upland grazing and cultivated land or even, on North Ronaldsay (no. 35), to confine sheep to the foreshore away from the cultivated interior of the island. The Feelie Dyke on Fair Isle clearly separates the hill grazing from the arable lands of the southern part of the island (see section 2), whereas the two treb dykes of North Ronaldsay must be ancient territorial boundaries (no. 35). On the whole, the latter type of massive dyke appears to be considerably older than the hill-dykes, even though their local terminology sometimes makes the distinction confusing: feelie or turf hill-dykes can also in Shetland be called gorsties, a term used of the older treb dykes such as the Funzie Girt on Fetlar (HU616930-626944). Treb dykes in Orkney may also be known as gairsties. The treb dykes are difficult to date, but the fact that they appear to be

Planticrues, Loch of Huxter, Whalsay

Funzie Girt, Fetlar

excavate. Salt was normally made in small quantities in a domestic context by evaporation over the kitchen fire.

Another product of the sea was for a time a vital factor in Orcadian economy: seaweed. This was gathered in vast quantities, dried and then burned in shallow pits until it became a boiling liquid; when the liquid cooled and hardened, it could be raised as a solid whole and broken into lumps ready for transport and sale as kelp, a valuable source of iodine and potassium salts. Kelp production was specially suited to Orkney with its shallow seas and prolific growth of seaweed, and it was never as important an industry in Shetland. The 18th century was the heyday of kelp-making when it was used extensively in the production of glass, soap and dyes, but it continued on a minor scale into this century. The over-grown remains of kelp-burning pits can be seen in many places round the shores of Orkney: they were circular, about 1.5 m in diameter and 0.6 m deep, lined and paved with stones (typically the Shetland kilns were different in shape, rectangular like those used in the Hebrides). There is a group of very well-preserved pits on the Crook Beach in the northern part of Sanday (HY 679459).

The use of lime for fertilising the fields led to the construction of drystone lime kilns, of which a few examples survive, usually built near the shore or near a loch, close to a limestone quarry. They were tall circular structures in which alternate layers of peat (as fuel) and limestone broken into small lumps were burned; the remains of two early 19th century kilns survive at Fladdabister (HU 437321), which supplied Lerwick and southern Shetland, and a later 19th century, well-preserved kiln may be seen at Lunna (HU 484693; see no. 43).

Shetland's easily quarried soapstone was the basis of a most important manufacturing industry in the Viking age and in prehistoric times and will be discussed later in connection with later prehistoric monuments.

Rural Industry

There are few monuments surviving by which the various rural industries of the Northern Isles may be traced. In the Eday excursion, attention has been drawn to the remains of the 17th century saltworks on the Calf of Eday, more because they are very unusual than because they are either well-preserved or typical monuments—this would be an interesting site to

earlier than tunship divisions, which may themselves relate to pre-Norse land divisions, has led to the suggestion recently that they might originate in the 1st millennium BC.

Bishop Reid's Tower, Kirkwall (no. 41)

Muness Castle, Unst (no. 38)

South Voe Croft Museum (no. 26)

Scalloway Castle (no. 37)

Lunna Church, Shetland (no. 43)

St Magnus Cathedral, Kirkwall (no. 49)

26* South Voe Croft Museum, Shetland

19th century AD.

HU 398146. Near the S tip of Shetland, some 5 km N of Sumburgh Airport, on a minor road to the E of the A 970; signposted.

The restored buildings that form this museum include not only the immediate steading with its house, byre and barn but also a typical corn mill, and the whole complex allows a fascinating insight into rural life in Shetland a hundred years ago. The furniture and fittings are mostly original to the house, but many smaller items have come from the collections of the Shetland Museum. The various components of the farmstead were built as conjoining units, aligned downslope to help drainage from the byre set at the lower end of the dwelling range. A cross-passage between the byre and the living-room provides access as well to the barn built alongside the north wall of the house—with another door in the opposite wall of the barn to create the cross-draught necessary for winnowing. The circular corn-drying kiln is at the upper end of the barn, and a storeroom at the lower end. At the upper end of the house, beyond the living-room, there is the bedroom with a wooden box bed and a wooden cradle. Both the dwelling range and the adjoining barn are roofed with thatch over a timber frame, held against the wind by ropes and stone weights. The west gable of the dwelling range incorporates a stone-built chimney, but there is an interesting reconstruction of a thatched smokehole midway between the two gables which served the original living-room hearth.

A path leads downhill to the south-east to the mill (HU 401145), the lowest of three clack mills on a tiny burn running fast down to the sea. Though very small, it would be quite adequate in performance and has been restored to working order—like the farmstead, its roof is thatched and held by stone weights.

South Voe Croft Museum (no. 26)

Watermill, South Voe Croft Museum (no. 26)

E

Corrigall Farm Museum (no. 27): stables and barn

27* Corrigall Farm Museum, Orkney

18th-19th centuries AD.

HY 324193. On the A 986 between Dounby and the junction with the A 965 Kirkwall to Stromness road, take a minor road near Harray Stores eastwards; signposted.

The range of buildings belonging to this steading date from the mid 18th century, and they have been beautifully restored to evoke a strong sense of farming

life in the mid 19th century (the farm was inhabited until the mid 20th century, when its potential for the creation of a rural museum was recognised, and it was bought by Orkney County Council). Not only has the fabric of the buildings been restored, but they have also been furnished with contemporary fittings and equipment typical of 19th century life—you are likely to find a resident hen, to see Orkney cheeses maturing and fish drying, and to smell the peat burning on the hearth. In 1981, the museum won the Award of the Association for the Preservation of Rural Scotland 'as a particularly fine example of restoration work in a rural setting'.

The three major buildings form a close-knit group running parallel to each other, with paving between them: the dwelling range, a barn and stable range and a separate byre. It is likely that the west end of the dwelling was originally a byre, but, by the mid 19th century, it had become a parlour with adjacent kitchen, living room and bedroom. The byre is furnished with stone partition-slabs, forming stalls, and a central drain, accommodating the cattle over the winter. The original stable for the native small horses is attached to the south side of the barn, with a manger built into the wall at either end, but the adoption of larger work horses in the 19th century led to the provision of a larger stable at the east end of the barn, which has timber-built stalls. The barn itself was primarily concerned with the preparation of grain for grinding into flour: a clay floor where the grain was threshed, opposing doorways to create the through-draught for winnowing, and a circular kiln for drying the grain. All the roofs consist of flagstones on a timber frame, covered with an insulating layer of turf.

The steading is well placed, with the Burn of Corrigall nearby to provide a source of water not only for domestic use but also, by the later 19th century, for a separate threshing mill powered by a water-wheel, the water for which was carried in an unusual aqueduct over the burn.

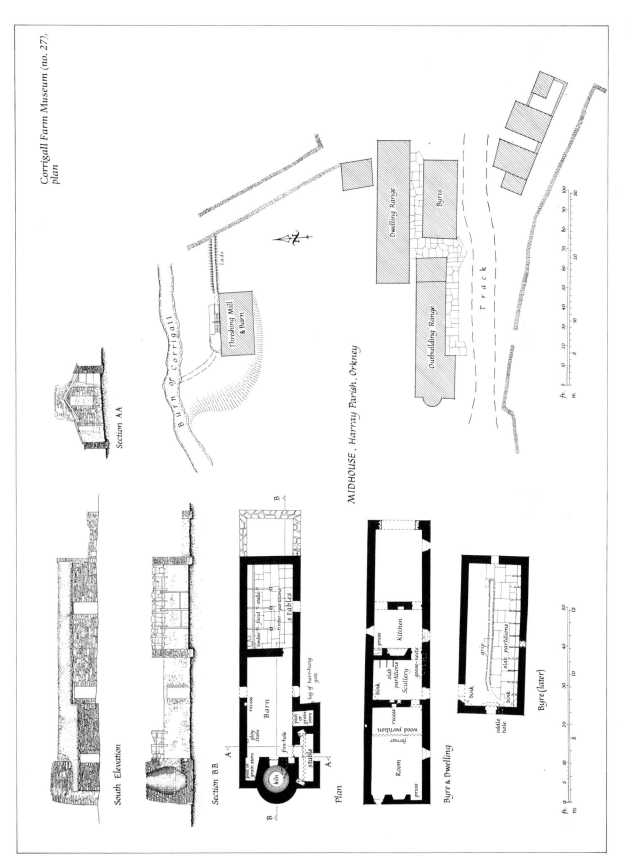

Corrigall Farm Museum (no. 27), plan

Section AA

South Elevation

Section B.B

Plan

MIDHOUSE, Harray Parish, Orkney

Byre & Dwelling

Byre (later)

Burn or Corrigall

Threshing Mill & Barn

lade

Dwelling Range

Byres

Outbuilding Range

Track

Barn

kiln

fire-hole

stable

pit or grain store

glug stane

recess

timber-faced stalls

timber partitions

stables

lug of harr-hung gate

pit or grain store

Room

former wood partition

press

recess

bink

slab partitions

Scullery

Kitchen

press

goose-nests

bink

oddle hole

bink

grip

slab partitions

bink

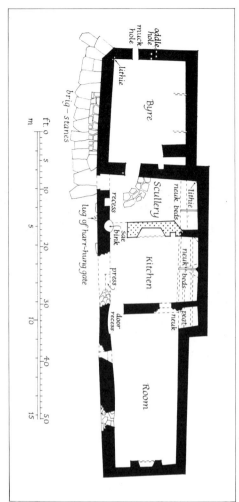

Mossetter (no. 28): entrance and neuk-beds in scullery

Plan of Mossetter farmhouse, Orkney (no. 28)

28 Mossetter, Farm Steading, Orkney

18th century AD.
HY 390197. About 5.5 km N of Finstown on the A 966, take a track E towards the Loch of Brockan for less than 1 km, then fork to the N.

This farm was abandoned around 1920, and it is now roofless, but it has some interesting features typical of older longhouses. It was built as a three-roomed house on a slope, with the byre at the downhill, western end, and the bedroom at the uphill end, and it was formerly roofed with flagstones and turf. There appear to have been only two small windows, both in the south wall of the bedroom.

Family and beasts used the same entrance, and a low curving stone wall directed the cattle into the byre rather than allowing them into the dwelling; the byre has lost its slab partitions, but both oddle-hole and muck-hole survive in the west end-wall. The central living-room has been divided into scullery and kitchen by an inserted chimney-wall, and the west gable of the bedroom has another fireplace. Along the north wall of the house there projects an outshot, running the length of scullery and kitchen and overlapping the bedroom, providing neuk-beds and, in the bedroom, a peat-neuk. The two neuk-beds in the kitchen are divided by an upright slab with horizontal corbelling above, a feature very reminiscent of the internal divisions in the broch at Midhowe (no. 59) and underlining the continuity of building traditions. Similarly archaic features are the recesses built into the south wall of the scullery, one low down to house the goose on her nest and the other rounded with a projected curved stone shelf for the water barrel.

Close by the old house, there are later outbuildings as well as traces of rig cultivation and old field-dykes.

29* Kirkbister, Farm Steading, Orkney

AD 1723.

HY 283253. About 4.5 km N of Dounby on the A 986, take the minor road to the NE for 1 km, then take the N fork, signposted.Orkney Islands Council.

It is unusual to be able to date an old farm so precisely, and the fact that the date is carved on the marriage lintel above the main door reflects the status of this farm: there was no question here of living under the same roof as the cattle. The walls are unusually high and the house is reasonably well lit by windows, and yet it has undergone remarkably little alteration for a house inhabited until recent times. Its linear range consists of four rooms, of which the kitchen is by far

the most interesting, because it was never divided and it retains the free-standing hearth with its stone-built fire-back. The wooden smoke-hole in the roof above has been reconstructed faithfully to the original, and the iron fittings by which cooking pots were suspended above the fire are still fixed to the charred beam above. The peat was kept in a neuk in the wall, the floor well-paved and the fire-back was kept whitewashed. In the south wall, close to the warmth of the fire, there is a beautifully constructed neuk-bed, not housed in a projecting outshot but contained within the thickness of the wall; two large flagstones form the front of the bed, with masonry above, and the neuk would have been snugly lined with wood.

The outbuildings include a barn with a well-preserved corn-drying kiln, a pigsty and a forge.

Kirkbister farm steading, Orkney (no. 29): kitchen with fire-back and neuk-bed

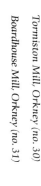

30* Tormiston Mill, Orkney

Early-mid 19th century AD.
HY 319125. On the A 965 Kirkwall to Stromness road, about 4 km SW of Finstown; signposted, now a restaurant and craft shop.

This elegant vertical-wheeled mill has been restored and adapted very successfully as a restaurant and craft shop, the use of natural wood and bare stone retaining an impression internally of the original three-storey mill, and the external appearance excellently preserved with an eight-spoke iron water-wheel, more than 4 m in diameter, and an unusual stone aqueduct carrying the water past the mill. With the prehistoric tomb of Maes Howe across the road, this is a very attractive place to linger on a tour of Orkney's mainland monuments.

31* Boardhouse Mill, Orkney

18th–19th centuries AD.
HY 254274. Beside the A 967 from Stromness to Birsay, about 1.5 km SE of Birsay village; signposted.

The three mills surviving at Boardhouse today are themselves the descendants of earlier mills on the burn running from the Loch of Boardhouse to the sea in the Bay of Birsay (see no. 39), and they are fine representatives of a long tradition of milling in what has always been one of the most fertile areas of Orkney. The youngest mill is still working commercially and is particularly well known for its production of beremeal (open to visitors June–August).

The new Barony Corn Mill was the last to be built, and it is a very large three-storey block with a large kiln vent at the apex of the roof, which was completed in 1873; it has three pairs of great millstones, all driven by an iron water-wheel, over 4 m in diameter, with wooden buckets. This replaced the Old Barony Corn Mill built in the 18th century, the fabric of which is still in good condition although the water-wheel is incomplete. The third, smaller building is a threshing mill, and it retains its water-wheel intact.

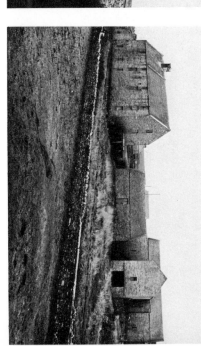

Tormiston Mill, Orkney (no. 30)

Boardhouse Mill, Orkney (no. 31)

Boardhouse Mill: mill-wheel
(no. 31)

Boardhouse Mill: first-floor
interior of New Barony Corn Mill
(no. 31)

32 Huxter, Clack Mills, Shetland

18th–19th century AD.

HU 172571. Take the A 971 from Lerwick to Sandness; about 1 km before the road terminates at the pier at Melby, fork W on a side road to Huxter. From the road end, walk W along between the houses and the sea and across a field to the burn.

The burn runs only a short distance from a small loch to the sea, but it falls steeply in its lower reaches, creating ideal conditions for small mills, and the loch itself has an excellent feeder burn that falls from a height of some 200 m in the hills to the south-east. There are three mills in the steeply-cut lower reaches of the burn, the last of which went out of regular use during World War II but was kept in good order until recently.

Each mill is arranged identically on the burn: the mill itself is built astride the direct route of the water-course, with a wide meander round it on the west side into which the water could be diverted, when the mill was idle, by means of sluice-gates. The timber gates are missing but their vertical slots are visible. Each rectangular building is about 5.5 m by 3 m, with an entrance only 0.6 m wide in the east gable, and the roof surviving on the lowest mill consists of heather thatch over turf and branches carried on a wooden frame—the little window over the door of this mill is very unusual and likely to have been a late modification. This last mill still has its millstones, and all three have remains of their horizontal wooden water-wheels, that in the uppermost mill retaining six of its original nine blades or feathers. The lades are beautifully constructed with stone linings, feeding the water into wooden chutes which direct it on to the inclined feathers of the wheels.

It is worth following the burn up to the Loch of Huxter to see the well-constructed stone dam and concrete sluice-gate setting, the stones for the dam almost certainly robbed from the adjacent broch. The latter has a recent sheep stell built on top of it, but the outer base of the broch wall is visible on the loch side, the broch entrance with a lintel still in position is incorporated into the stell, and, on the south side, the sheep are clearly using the broch entrance passage and the entrance into a guard cell as a means of getting in and out of the stell. To the south of the loch are two burnt mounds which, unusually, have been given names: Little Brownie's Knowe (HU 173566) and Muckle (Big) Brownie's Knowe (HU 171563). There is a magnificent view to the north of the island of Papa Stour, on which an important late Norse settlement has been discovered and partially excavated at Da Biggins.

33 Troswick, Clack Mills, Shetland

18th–19th century AD.

HU 405172–409167. On the A 970 Lerwick to Sumburgh road, some 9 km N of Sumburgh, take a minor road SSE to the Loch of Clumlie.

From the road at the south end of the loch, the line of mills astride the Clumlie Burn is a fine sight, falling away south-south-eastwards to the sea. There are nine mills in all, mostly quite ruinous except for the lowest building which was restored in 1929 and is still in working order, with a 12-feathered tirl (this latter mill may be visited by taking the road to Troswick Farm down the north-east side of the burn). Between the loch and the road, in a very boggy area at the head of the burn, there are the remains of two, probably successive, dams, the larger retaining the groove for its sluice-gate and the smaller having a wooden frame for the gate.

opening or winnowing hole in the opposite wall to create a through draught. There is another unusual feature in the tirl, which has two rows of blades, one set above the other making a total of 12 blades. The mill was said to grind about a bushel of grain per hour (about 250 kilograms).

34 Dounby, Click Mill, Orkney

Early 19th century AD.
HY 325228. From Dounby in central N mainland, take the B 9057 for almost 4 km; signposted. HBM (SDD).

This mill is the only standing example of a horizontal watermill in Orkney, and it has been excellently restored with all its machinery in working order and its flagstone roof intact. It was built around 1823 to replace an older mill in the same place, Millbrig, and it was used throughout most of the rest of that century; it has been necessary to engineer a piped supply of water so that the restored mill can operate for about 8 minutes at a time, because the original water supply was destroyed by quarrying in the burn for stones for road-making in the 1920s.

The building is very small, only about 4.5 m by 2 m, with the entrance in one of the long walls with a small

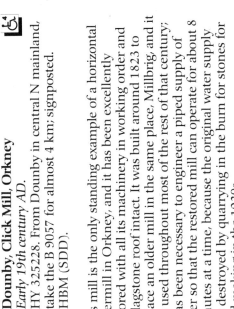

Dounby watermill, Orkney: interior (no. 34)

35 North Ronaldsay Dykes, Orkney

19th century AD and earlier.
HU 7654. The island can be reached by sea or by air from Kirkwall.

The island of North Ronaldsay is famous both for its sheep and for its sheep dyke. The sheep are of a very old native breed and they feed chiefly on seaweed, being confined to the foreshore by a stone dyke, some 1.5 m high, which encircles the entire 19 km perimeter of the island. The original 19th century building and continuing maintenance of the dyke represent communal labour by the islanders, and the whole method of sheep husbandry here is an invaluable and almost unique survival of a once widespread communal system of agriculture.

Equally interesting are the two earthen dykes, the Matches Dyke (HY 756546–767544) and the Muckle Gairsty (HY 750534–768521), which run roughly east-west across the island dividing it into three unequal parts. Local legend attributes the dykes to a man who divided the land between his three sons, apparently according to the old udal system of inheritance; whether or not the legend is true, the two dykes are almost certainly territorial boundaries of some sort. Their date is uncertain: they appear on a map published around 1770 but they could well be very much earlier, perhaps prehistoric in origin. There is a particularly well-preserved length of the Muckle Gairsty running south-south-eastwards from Northness in the south-east tip of the island (HY 766527–768522), where it is 4 m wide and almost 2 m high.

6

MEDIEVAL PALACES AND CASTLES

Orkney is fortunate in having a rare well-preserved and indisputable Norse castle of the 12th century on the small island of Wyre (no. 42). There follows a near gap in the record of surviving monuments of some 400 years before the main period of building castles and defensive residences begins in the Northern Isles in the late 16th century, from which have survived some exceptional monuments, culminating in the splendour of the Earl's Palace in Kirkwall. They demonstrate that Orkney and Shetland shared in the architectural developments taking place on mainland Scotland and in some cases excelled in their architectural refinements. A castle that no longer survives is that commemorated in Castle Street, Kirkwall, where Earl Henry Sinclair built a castle in the late 14th century facing St Magnus Cathedral; it was demolished in 1615, though parts of its walls were still in existence until the later 19th century. It was said to have been a particularly strongly built castle. By the mid 16th century, one very popular design for a stone-built fortification consisted of a main rectangular block with towers attached to two diagonally opposite corners (known to architectural historians as the Z-plan), and there are good examples of this design at Muness (no. 38) and Scalloway (no. 40) in Shetland and Noltland in Orkney (no. 37). The towers not only provided extra accommodation but also added to the defensive potential of the building, allowing more effective coverage of the ground immediately surrounding the building. A great asset was the fact

that the entrance could be placed at the angle between a tower and the main block, thus protecting it from several directions by means of small openings for hand-guns.

There seems to have been a strong element of fashion rather than necessity dictating the extent to which castle-design included gun-loops and shot-holes. At this stage in the development of hand-guns, they were in practice almost ludicrously ineffective compared with the longbow or the cross-bow, either of which was much faster to load and more accurate; it has been estimated that the hakbut might fire six or seven one-ounce balls *per hour*, a sad contrast to the twelve arrows per minute of which a good longbowman was capable. Seen in this light, one can appreciate that the tiers of gun-loops at Noltland Castle were perhaps more effective as a psychological deterrent than as a practical battery.

The castles at Scalloway and Muness in Shetland were both built of rubble with harled exteriors and dressed stone blocks where required for door and window openings, external corners and decorative features. The basic materials apart from the freestone dressings were of local origin as were, reluctantly, the labourers who were obliged not only to work but to feed themselves at their own communal expense. It is thought that the two castles may have been designed by the same man, probably the Earl's Master of Work,

Earl's Palace, Kirkwall (no. 36)

Andrew Crawford, who was also responsible for the Palace at Kirkwall. Muness is the more refined and in some ways architecturally advanced of the two, even to the extent of having had glass in its windows rather than iron grilles, despite the lesser importance of its owner (though Earl Patrick was probably not often in residence at Scalloway).

Muness and Scalloway share with the Earl's Palace at Kirkwall a decorative device special to the Northern Isles at this period: the projecting tiers of masonry supporting turrets have imitation shot-holes alternating with the corbels. They can be seen particularly well on the Earl's Palace where they are closer to the ground than elsewhere.

Earl's Palace, Kirkwall (no. 36)

Earl's Palace, Kirkwall: great hall (no. 36)

The entrance of the great hall on the first-floor is flanked on the left by a small vaulted room, used by the Earl's major-domo, and on the right by a tiny and very attractive room interpreted as an ante-chamber for guests waiting to see the Earl. It has a stone basin in a recess just inside the entrance arch, and its barrel-vaulted ceiling has panels of fine masonry separated by moulded and decorative stone ribs.

36* Earl's Palace, Kirkwall, Orkney

AD 1606.
HY 449107. In the centre of the town, close to St Magnus Cathedral.
HBM (SDD).

This building has been described as 'possibly the most mature and accomplished piece of Renaissance architecture left in Scotland', and it is certainly a most attractive monument set amongst trees and well-kept lawns. It was known as the New Wark of the Yards when first built, to distinguish it from the older Bishop's Palace, then known as the Place of the Yards.

As it survives, it is an L-shaped building of two main blocks with a short wing projecting from the north-west corner of the main block, but it seems originally to have conformed to a courtyard plan, though nothing is known of the character of the west and north sides, or if indeed they were ever completed. The ground-floor consists of vaulted storerooms, a vaulted kitchen and a splendidly spacious main stairway leading to the 'state apartments' on the first floor. Traces of a second floor survive very incompletely. The outstanding features of the Palace are the main entrance, the oriel windows and the great fireplace in the hall, but there are many other interesting details.

The great hall is still a magnificent though roofless chamber, and it is easy to imagine its impact when inhabited, full of people and colour and urgent conversation. It is fully 16.5 m long and 6 m wide, requiring two fireplaces and several fine windows, including a huge window in the south gable with triple round-headed lights. The larger fireplace on the west side of the hall has truly noble proportions: flanked by moulded jambs echoing those of the main entrance, the fireplace is framed by a straight arch some 5 m long, above which there is an arch designed to lessen the strain of the weight of masonry above. The capitals of the jambs on either side are embellished with an earl's coronet and the initials P E O for Patrick, Earl of Orkney. It is recorded that several rooms of the palace were 'curiously painted with Scripture stories', like the Earl's Palace at Birsay (no. 39), and it is likely that the great hall was one of those rooms, perhaps with a painted ceiling.

37 Scalloway Castle, Shetland

AD 1599
HU 402393. In Scalloway, beside the harbour, some 10 km from Lerwick on the A 970; signposted.
HBM (SDD).

The basic design of this castle consists of a rectangular main block, some 18 m by 10 m, with an 8 m square tower at its south-west angle, built with three upper floors; the roof and flooring of the two uppermost

The main entrance, set at the angle of two wings, is badly weathered but still conveys a strong sense of its former grandeur; there is a Doric element in the deeply moulded half-columns flanking the door, and the capitals were once richly decorated, as were the surrounds of the three panels above the door. The lower panel held an inscription originally, the middle panel displayed the arms of Earl Patrick, and the uppermost panel the royal arms of Scotland, both now barely discernible. Another inscribed panel was set above the corbelled chimney-breast on the adjacent wall. The door itself would have consisted of an outer wooden door and an inner iron gate or yett.

storeys no longer survive, but the building is otherwise in good condition. The doorway on the ground floor of the tower is sited strategically close to the angle between tower and main block, with a covering gun-port beside it. Although many have been altered since, all the windows were originally furnished with shot-holes for hand weapons. Above the door are very weathered panels, the uppermost containing an armorial carving and the main lower panel an inscription which commemorated Earl Patrick and bore a Latin couplet:

'The house whose foundation is rock will stand,
But will perish, if built upon shifting sand.'

The tower is mostly taken up by the stairway and landings, and the major rooms are in the main block. A large kitchen, with a massive fireplace and a well, and a storeroom occupy the ground floor, while the whole of the first floor is taken up by a spacious hall served by nine windows and two fireplaces, with an arched recess in the north wall which probably held a dresser. The second floor was divided into two rooms and the third into three rooms, all with fireplaces and windows and, in the case of the second-floor rooms, with private garderobes or toilets. There were also small chambers on the upper floors in the tower and the corner turrets. Externally the turrets provide the only areas of decoration in their corbelled footings.

Scalloway Castle was built in 1600 by Earl Patrick, but it declined in importance after his execution 15 years later. It was garrisoned briefly by Cromwell's troops, and thereafter fell into increasing disrepair until taken into state guardianship in 1908. An account written in 1701 mentions traces of decorative wall paintings still to be seen, and gives us a glimpse of the original colourful splendour of the building.

38 Muness Castle, Unst, Shetland

AD 1598.
HP 629011. SE tip of Unst, some 4 km along minor road from Uyeasound.
HBM (SDD).

It is fitting that the most northerly castle in Britain should also be an exceptionally fine architectural achievement. It is a small and beautifully proportioned defensive residence, compact and suited to the needs of a laird's family and yet up-to-date with fashionable details current at the end of the 16th century.

In its basic design the castle forms an elongated rectangle, 22.3 m by 7.9 m, with a circular tower at each of the north and south corners, the south tower being slightly larger than the north tower. The ground floor and the first floor survive virtually intact, but the second floor and roof were demolished many years ago and the stone used to build the modern wall surrounding the castle. There were small turrets at the west and east corners of the missing third floor, for the corbelling that supported them is still visible, adding a decorative note to the upper part of the castle which may originally have been echoed by an ornamental corbel-course at eaves level. The roof itself is likely to have been gabled.

The entrance is at ground-level on the south-west side of the building; the original stonework of the doorway had been removed, but the doorway inserted in recent years came from a farmhouse at Lund and may well originally have belonged to the castle. There are two original carved panels above the entrance: one records the building of the castle by Laurence Bruce in 1598, and the other bears his arms and initials. The severity of the lower part of the castle walls is tempered by small windows, shot-holes and gun-ports which show considerable variety in the design of their stonework, especially the shot-holes and gun-ports which are both functional and decorative.

Inside the castle, the ground floor contains three storerooms and a large kitchen, all with vaulted ceilings, as well as two small rooms in the towers. The kitchen has a huge fireplace, with a circular oven built into its back wall, and a sink in one corner. On the first floor, reached by a spacious stairway, there is a large central hall with a fireplace (and a small alcove in the side of the fireplace where the salt could be kept dry), flanked on either side by smaller rooms whose fireplaces were in the gable walls. The south-east room is served by an extra stair from the storeroom below, but the north-west room can be entered only from the hall. This would be the laird's private quarters, with an extra room in the adjoining tower and a small stair to a room above. From what survives of the second floor, it is possible to see that there were again three main

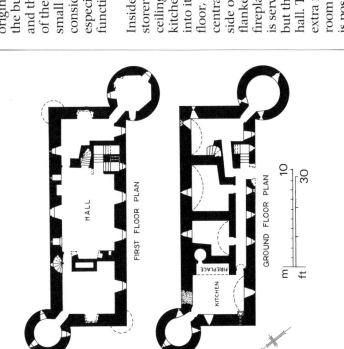

Plan of Muness Castle, Unst (no. 38)

Muness Castle, Unst: armorial panel and inscription above entrance (no. 38)

Muness Castle, Unst: corbelling beneath angle turret (no. 38)

rooms together with the chambers in the towers, completing a very comfortable and spacious residence, which would undoubtedly have had interior decoration and furnishings to match the refinement of the building.

As might be expected at this period, Muness was built not by a Shetlander but by a Scotsman. Laurence Bruce came from Perthshire, but because he was a half-brother of Robert Stewart, Earl of Orkney and Shetland, he acquired lands in Unst and the means to

build a fine castle there. The poem carved above the entrance shows his pride in the castle:

'Listen you to know this building who began
Laurence the Bruce he was that worthy man
Who earnestly his heirs and offspring prays
To help and not to hurt this work always.'

The building was indeed cared for and completed by his son, Andrew Bruce, but it was attacked and burned by a foreign privateer force only 29 years after building began.

Earl's Palace, Birsay (no. 39)

39 Earl's Palace, Birsay, Orkney ♿
16th century AD.
HY 248277. In the village of Birsay, close by the
A 966.
HBM (SDD).

The striking but gaunt shell of the Earl's Palace still
dominates the village and the broad bay of Birsay, and
the walls convey a strong sense of its original massive
grandeur, but it takes a little imagination to restore an
impression of its once magnificent elegance: it was
described in 1633 as 'a sumptuous and stately
dwelling'. The rooms on the upper floor were
attractively decorated with painted ceilings, including
biblical scenes with appropriate texts, and they would
undoubtedly have been furnished with brightly

coloured wall-hangings. The exterior of the building seems always to have been fairly austere—it was after all a fortified residence of the Earl of Orkney—but the upper windows of the north and east wings were embellished with carved and pinnacled pediments.

It was built by Robert Stewart, Earl of Orkney, in the latter half of the 16th century as a courtyard house in fashionable Renaissance style, consisting of four wings round a rectangular courtyard with square towers at each corner except that on the north-west. It seems that a decision to modify the original plan was made during the course of a long building programme, because the north wing is awkwardly placed, masking the gable-end of the west wing and very close to the west side of the tower at the north-east corner, as if there was originally to have been only a screen-wall along the north side of the courtyard (and presumably a tower at the north-west corner to match the other three). The fact that the upper-floor windows on the north and east wings match suggests that this change of design took place not long after the completion of the latter wing. In the centre of the courtyard is a circular well. The external walls of the Palace are lined with gun-loops, as were the internal walls lining the courtyard, including one surviving on the west wing which is angled to cover the main entrance into the courtyard from outside. The ground-floor was lit by small horizontal windows as an additional defensive precaution. The entire building was two-storeyed except for the north-east tower which rose an extra storey, but only the towers, the north wing and part of the west wing survive to any height, for it has been uninhabited since the late 17th century.

There exists a beautifully detailed plan of the Palace, drawn in the 17th century, which shows not only the missing upper storeys but the main entrance with the initials R E O for Robert Earl of Orkney and the date 1574 above what may be either a window or, more probably, an armorial panel. It also shows the immediate setting of the Palace: the pathway leading

out to Skipi Geo to the north where boats were landed, huge peat-stacks on the west between the Palace and the shore of the bay and a range of walled enclosures down the east side of the building, including a 'Floure Yard' or flower garden and a 'Herbe Yard'. The 'Bow Butts' ran the length of these two gardens, so that the ladies could admire the archers at their target practice—and there was a bowling green in front of the Palace.

The drawing also shows the church and churchyard close to the south-west corner of the Palace. This had been built in 1664 as a cruciform church (possibly on the site of an 11th century church) but it was demolished and re-built in 1760 as the simple rectangular church that survives as the parish church in use today. Some earlier features were re-used: the 17th century belfry that crowns the west gable and, in the south wall, a lancet window of which the upper part is 13th century work. The sill is in fact part of an inscribed lintel, and another fragment of the same lintel was re-used as a window-jamb in a cottage just north of the church: together they read MONS BELLUS, the name that was used in the 16th century for the Birsay residence of the Bishop of Orkney. That bishop's palace no longer survives, but architectural fragments have been dug up around the church and adjacent gardens which may belong either to the church and bishop's palace or to the earlier church. It has also been suggested that the bishop's palace was incorporated into the Earl's Palace.

The bridge over the Barony burn has a longer history than is immediately apparent. It is a stone-built bridge with two arches and, although the upper part may well be medieval—a two-span bridge is certainly shown on an 18th century drawing and a bridge on the same spot on the 17th century drawing already mentioned. A bridge over the burn was vital to access from Kirkwall and elsewhere on mainland, unlike the modern approach from the north-east of the Palace.

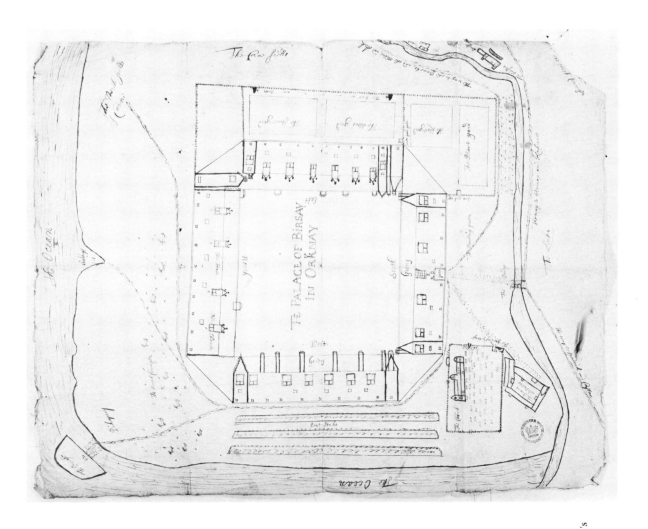

17th century drawing of the Earl's Palace, Birsay (no. 39), held by Scottish Record Office (RHP 35836)

Noltland Castle, Westray (no. 40)

40* Noltland Castle, Westray, Orkney

16th century AD.

HY 429486. Close to the road, 800 m W of Pierowall.

HBM (SDD).

The siting of this most impressive castle emphasises the importance in former times of the natural harbour at Pierowall, and the height of the parapet provides an extensive view of the northern isles of Orkney. Most of the building uses the local grey flagstone but the finer stonework consists of red sandstone which was probably imported from Eday, a short voyage to the south-east of Westray. Though roofless, the castle survives in good condition, despite the fact that it was never completed, and it is an excellent example of a 16th century Z-plan design with a central block and two towers. Most remarkable of all is the number of gun-loops, no fewer than 71 arranged in tiers, making it an unusually fortified building—or at least an unusually fearsome building, which was probably their prime purpose.

The main rectangular block measures 26.5 m by 11 m and, though incomplete, was designed to have three upper storeys, with square towers at its south-west and north-east angles, the south-west tower slightly bigger at 9 m square than the north-east tower, presumably because it enclosed not only the entrance but the main stairway. Although initially the castle looks very severe, there are decorative details; the lower string-course on the south-west tower is moulded and bears traces of carving, while the moulded panel above the doorway would originally have held a carved armorial panel; at the wall-head there were once turrets and a parapet walk, and the decorative projecting corbels that supported them may still be seen; the gables were stepped. And the inside of the castle, at least on the upper floors, must have been quite elegant to judge from the proportions of the main hall and the spacious design of the stairway, one of the finest of its period in Scotland, leading from the entrance up to the hall—the central newel of the stair is finished at the top with a great carved stone terminal. The hall may also be reached by a back stair from the kitchen below to a small servery where finishing touches might be added to meals about to be served in the great hall (a convenience not matched by conditions in the kitchen, which must have been very dark and stuffy). The basement was originally divided into two levels by a wooden floor creating storerooms between the kitchen and the vaulted stone ceiling that supports the hall and chamber on the first floor. The passion for gun-loops, which are such a feature of the castle, even extended to placing two in the wall at the back of the huge fireplace in the kitchen.

On the first floor were not only the hall and the laird's private apartments but also, beside the stair in the south-west tower, a small chamber that seems to have acted as a strong-room, because there are lockers with secret compartments built into the sills of the two windows. It is also worth examining the gun-loops in the basement, because many have slots designed to hold wooden mountings for the guns.

Noltland Castle, Westray: main stair (no. 40)

Noltland Castle, Westray: carved newel above main stair (no. 40)

The courtyard on the south side of the castle with its arched gateway and foundations of domestic buildings is a later addition, described in an 18th century document as a 'garden'. The castle itself was built sometime between 1560 and 1574 by Gilbert Balfour, a Scot from Fife with a particularly ruthless personal history, who had acquired through marriage lands in Westray in 1560. Despite the fact that Noltland was never properly finished, it was used for at least two centuries both as a military stronghold and as a residence.

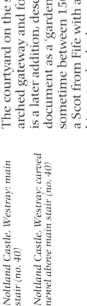

41* Bishop's Palace, Kirkwall, Orkney

12th–17th centuries AD.
HY 449108. At the corner of Palace Road and Watergate.
HBM (SDID).

The Bishop's Palace is Kirkwall's oldest surviving secular building, although there has been some controversy in academic circles over just how old its foundations may be. Most of the building as it survives today dates from the time of Bishop Robert Reid in the mid 16th century, but it has been argued that the

86

*Bishop's Palace, Kirkwall:
Bishop Reid's tower (no. 41)*

*Bishop's Palace, Kirkwall:
interior with St Magnus Cathedral
beyond (no. 41)*

lowest part of the main block includes the remains of an earlier episcopal residence, perhaps that of Bishop William, under whom the seat of the bishopric was transferred from Birsay to Kirkwall to accompany the building of the new Cathedral in the mid 12th century. This early palace would have been a rectangular hall-house, with a ground-floor given over to storage and workrooms and a great hall on the first floor—the hall in which the Norwegian King Hakon died in 1263 after his crushing defeat in western Scotland at the Battle of Largs. Nothing remains of this hall-house above its basal courses, and even those are overshadowed by the rise in ground-level outside.

Bishop Reid's reconstruction of the building in the mid 16th century retained the basic design of first-floor hall and ground-floor storage, but he added the great round tower at the north-west corner, which contained five storeys (including his own personal apartments) and an attic, and another storey plus attic to the main block. The building thus became considerably more grand and ample in its accommodation. The weathered statue carved in white stone and set off by the red sandstone of its niche in the outer wall of the tower used to be thought to represent St Olaf, but is generally accepted now as the great Bishop Reid himself.

The details of the arrangement of rooms on the upper floors of the main block are uncertain, as only the shell of the building survives, and its analysis is further hampered by the fact that it was again modified, probably around 1600 by Earl Patrick as part of his own palace complex. Early drawings and accounts of the building make clear that there were, until about 1800, two square towers, apparently free-standing, close to its north-east end, nothing of which can now be seen.

The round tower is in itself an interesting structure and must originally have been a very imposing addition to the house. Although round externally, the rooms inside were approximately square, and the spiral stair rises within the thickness of the wall. The parapet is supported by decorative corbelling and the parapet-walk was originally roofed over, a very unusual design. The tower had a square cap-house rising above the level of the parapet-roof, with a small square room inside.

♿

42 Cubbie Roo's Castle, Wyre, Orkney
12th century AD.
HY 441262. On the NW side of the island, overlooking Wyre Sound; a walk of some 1.5 km from the jetty, by ferry from Tingwall.
HBM (SDD).

'At that time there was a very able man named Kolbein Hruga farming on Wyre in Orkney. He had a fine stone fort built there, a really solid stronghold'—so records *Orkneyinga Saga* of events around 1150, and the same castle is described as a difficult place to attack in 1231 in *Hakonar Saga*. Although in the past there has been controversy over its date, the small stone castle surviving on Wyre is now generally accepted as that built in the 12th century by Kolbein—whose Norse nickname would have been Kobbie or Kubbie, hence

the modern name. As such it is one of the earliest stone-built castles in Scotland and certainly the best preserved, having been excavated in the late 1920s and later consolidated.

In its original design, the castle consisted of an almost square keep, about 8 m across with mortared walls almost 2 m thick, surrounded at a distance of about 8 m by outer defences: a stone wall with an outer ditch and bank. Only the ground floor of the keep survives complete, but it must have risen at least two more floors to have achieved a good view over the island and the surrounding seaways; the narrow projecting ledge that supported the timber first floor can be seen on the inner face of the north wall. Access to the upper floors would have been by internal wooden ladders, and the sole entrance to the keep was at first-floor level, again reached by a retractable wooden ladder (although this doorway no longer survives, it was recorded in the late 17th century). The ground floor was probably used for storing supplies, as were those of later tower-houses, and a rectangular tank cut into the solid rock was presumably used either to store drinking water or to keep a living supply of fish. It is doubtful whether the keep was a permanent residence; it seems more likely that it was used as a refuge in times of trouble, for its size is quite unsuited to the establishment of an important Norse family, and the name of the adjacent modern farm, the Bu of Wyre, suggests the existence of a separate Norse farmstead with its great hall and outbuildings—and its church (see no. 51).

The enclosing defences survive only to the west, north and east of the keep, for elsewhere they have been obliterated by later building. The excavations identified at least five phases of subsequent building and modification around the keep, some of which may be as early as the 13th century, and the entire complex is testimony to the success of the original design—neither of the other two fortifications mentioned in *Orkneyinga Saga*, at Cairston near Stromness and on the island of Damsay, survived so long.

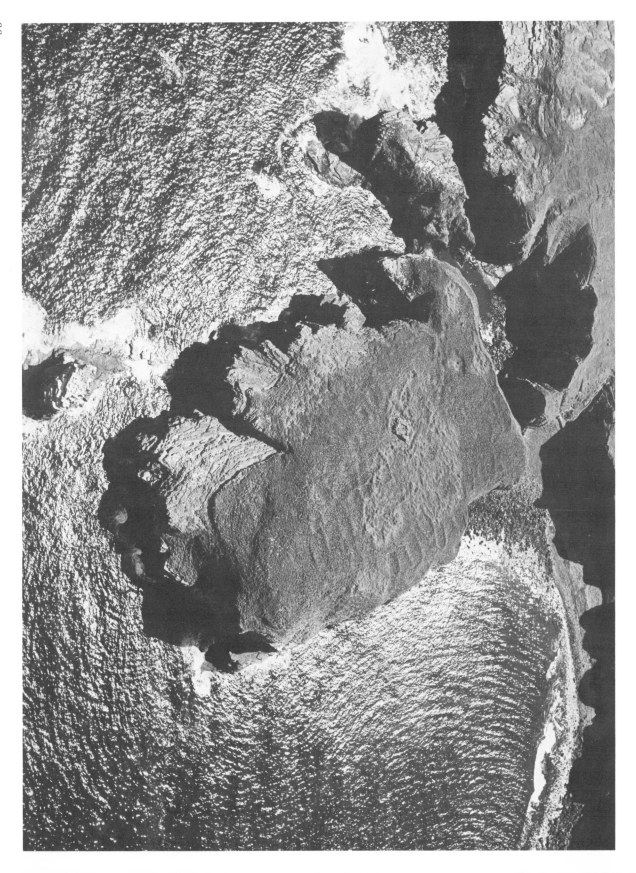

7

ECCLESIASTICAL MONUMENTS

The Reformation led to no major changes to the medieval churches of Orkney and Shetland, for their simple layout was easily adapted to congregational worship. At Pierowall (no. 45) the old chancel was replaced by a laird's aisle and the nave was widened, but in most cases there was no re-building—even the round church at Orphir survived until the latter part of the 18th century, its form perhaps well suited, if unorthodox, to the new ideas. Natural wastage coupled with sheer old age brought about the abandonment of many churches. The pity is that so many were then deliberately demolished in the late 18th century when new parish churches were built.

A number of finely carved, even elaborate, tombstones of the 16th century and later may be seen, some still in family burial aisles (eg no. 44), and in Shetland there are several interesting stones commemorating Hanseatic merchants and foreign seamen (eg no. 46). In the ruins of St Mary's Church, Cullingsburgh, Bressay (HU 521422), there are two 17th century tombstones, one bearing an inscription in Dutch to 'the brave commander', Claes Jansen Bruyn of Durgerdam, who served the Dutch East India Company. A number of 17th and 18th century tombstones are housed in an old turf-grown burial aisle in the churchyard at Tingwall (HU 418437), including that of Andrew Crawford, Master of Work to the Earl of Orkney and Shetland, who was responsible for the construction of the Earl's Palace at Kirkwall and probably the castles at Scalloway and Muness. The

burial vault with its finely moulded archway is all that remains of the earlier medieval church with its tall round tower. There is also, nearby in the churchyard, a 17th century stone sarcophagus, carved with emblems of mortality in relief and elegiac couplets on both long sides. This used to serve as a social resting-place for men who arrived early for the Sunday morning service, some of whom may have walked several miles—the tomb could seat up to eight people! A fine series of tombstones may be seen in St Magnus Cathedral (no. 49), including 17th century examples with particularly excellent lettering rivalled by two at Pierowall (no. 45).

The new churches of the 17th and 18th centuries were simple rectangular buildings, sometimes with a laird's aisle projecting from one long side to form a T-plan, eg St Olaf's Church, Voe (no. 44).

Medieval churches

The Northern Isles are fortunate in the number and variety of surviving medieval churches, even though St Magnus Cathedral in Kirkwall stands in a class of its own, there being no other building of remotely comparable architectural quality or elaboration. In Orkney particularly, there are several Romanesque churches of the 12th century which, though roofless, have well-preserved walls and architectural details. These are mostly characterised by rectangular naves and square-ended chancels, with round-arched

Brough of Deerness, Orkney, aerial view of chapel and house foundations

Tingwall, Shetland, sarcophagus in churchyard

doorways and windows, but there is one survivor of a group of churches with tall round towers: St Magnus Church on Egilsay (no. 50). Formerly there were similar churches, known as 'steeple-kirks', at Stenness and Deerness in Orkney (the latter with twin towers) and at Tingwall, Ireland and Papil in Shetland, most of which were demolished in the late 18th century. These round towers are very reminiscent of the free-standing towers of 9th-12th century Ireland, of which two examples were certainly built in central Scotland at Abernethy and Brechin, and they could well represent Irish influence on the Northern Isles.

At two Orcadian churches, Brough of Birsay (no. 57) and Eynhallow (no. 52), it is possible that there was once a square tower at the west end, reduced to its foundations at the first site and to a porch at the second. If these were towers, they might demonstrate continuing influence from Northumbria, and at Birsay

there is certainly Norwegian church design reflected in the circular altar recesses on either side at the eastern end of the nave.

As they survive today, these small medieval churches give an impression of bleak austerity, but their plain architecture would have been countered by colour and lightness in their interiors; and in some cases there was architectural embellishment in the form of stone-carving, since removed (eg Eynhallow, no. 52) or lost. Traces of plastering indicate that the rubble walls were smooth and light in colour (and may have been painted), and the stone dressings around doorways and windows in Orkney sometimes included red sandstone. Internal furnishings might include woven wall-hangings, carved and painted wooden fittings and silver chalices and candlesticks. Seating, if any, would be narrow stone or wooden benches set along the walls, such as still survive in stone on the Brough of Birsay (no. 57). Roofing would be flagstones, turf or thatch on a wooden frame.

A number of churches bear the name 'cross-kirk', but it implies dedication to the Holy Rude rather than architectural design as a cruciform church—although a few cruciform churches do seem to have existed, for example at Birsay in Orkney (demolished) and at Cullingsburgh on Bressay in Shetland (HU 521421; very ruinous).

Orphir church (no. 48) is the only surviving Scottish example of a design briefly fashionable in medieval western Europe; modelled on the Church of the Holy Sepulchre in Jerusalem, such round churches were built during the period of the Crusades to the Holy Land by returning crusaders or 'Jerusalem farers' as they are termed in runes inscribed inside Maes Howe (no. 95). The church at Orphir was part of an earl's estate, built close to the great hall, and other 12th century churches have proved to be part of great Norse family estates: the church on Wyre was built close to both the domestic farmstead and the castle (no. 42), while on Westray recent excavations have revealed a high status late Norse settlement at Tuquoy close to the contemporary Cross Kirk or Westside church (HY 455431, HBM, SDD). In Shetland, both Norse settlements and churches tend to be in coastal locations, exploiting both the better land and good harbours for fishing boats, and it is noticeable that the churches are very often not at the immediate head of the bay but just round to one side, so as not to occupy prime economic locations. A good example is St Mary's Church, Sand (HU 346472), overlooking Sand Voe, where the chancel arch is astoundingly intact whereas most of the rest of the church is reduced to its base-course.

Although the documentary and archaeological evidence is controversial, the buildings on Eynhallow (no. 52) may well have been a medieval monastery. To judge by known monasteries in other Atlantic Norse

colonies, such sites would look far more like normal farms than like the great monasteries of southern Scotland and England and would be correspondingly more difficult to recognise. The Brough of Deerness in Orkney was for a long time thought to be the site of a medieval monastery, but recent excavations have suggested that, although there is a small rectangular chapel of 12th century date, the surrounding houses are likely to be of secular rather than ecclesiastical nature, a situation parallel to that on the Brough of Birsay (no. 57).

The influences from eastern Scotland and north-east England on the architecture of St Magnus Cathedral are unmistakeable, and the same influences gave rise to an equally distinctive fashion in gravestones: the hogback monument. This is a recumbent stone placed lengthwise over the grave, shaped and carved to imitate a house with a curved roof-ridge, and it is a style that was invented in the 10th century by Scandinavian settlers in North Yorkshire. In Scotland, hogbacks are mostly found in central and eastern areas, no further north than Angus, and the group in the Northern Isles must represent direct contact by sea with these areas further south. Few monuments are still in their original positions, such as that in the churchyard of St Boniface on Papa Westray, Orkney (no. 54), and they are late examples dating to the 12th century by which time the roof-ridge had flattened and lost its characteristic curved hogback shape. Examples of true hogbacks of 11th century date may be seen in Tankerness House Museum in Kirkwall, found originally in St Olaf's Churchyard and beneath the chancel of St Magnus Cathedral. A small hogback, only 1.2 m long, was found on the west side of the church on St Ninian's Isle in Shetland (no. 47) and is now in Lerwick Museum; made of steatite, it is plain but well-shaped with a flattened ridge. The stone must have been transported to the island, probably in a finished state, from the Cunningsburgh area on the other side of mainland (see no. 56), which is the closest source of steatite, a variety of talc.

St Mary's Chapel, Sand, Shetland

43 Lunna Church, Shetland

18th century AD.

HU 485690. On the narrow neck of land leading to Lunna Ness, just to the E of the minor road leading N from the B 9071 at Vidlin on N mainland.

Still in use as the parish church, this building has a particularly light and attractive interior. It was built in 1753 possibly on medieval foundations by Robert Hunter of Lunna, and renovated both in 1830 and 1933, as a simple rectangular church with a porch–an oddity is the small annexe on the south side with a small opening into the church, which has been interpreted both as a 'squint' for the priest to keep an eye on the altar while resting and as a 'leper hole', a small opening in the wall of the church through which the afflicted could listen to the service and receive communion without distressing the rest of the congregation. Built into the wall of the porch are two 17th century graveslabs, which came from the Hunter family mausoleum that existed before the church was built. Inside the church, a fine 18th century memorial is set into the wall beside the pulpit.

Although no previous church was in use at Lunna in 1753, the existing church was not the first to be built here. Adjacent to the churchyard, and approached through an unexpectedly grand gateway, is a large irregular mound (probably of prehistoric origin) on which a chapel with an enclosure had been built, perhaps in the 12th century. Its foundations are clearly visible as a rectangular building with an entrance to the south-west, but it is not known when the church went out of use.

The imposing gateway is a landscape feature belonging to Lunna House, which overlooks the site, a 17th and 18th century house built as the seat of the Hunter family (now a hotel). Incorporated into the external front of the house is an armorial panel which has been moved from its original position: it commemorates the marriage in 1707 of Thomas Hunter and Grisella Bruce. The house was for a time the HQ of the Norwegian resistance movement in the Second World War, and the base for boats ferrying armaments and men across the North Sea to occupied Norway.

On the shore of West Lunna Voe is an excellent example of a circular beehive-shaped lime kiln (HU 484693), while further round the voe to the north is a superb prehistoric burnt mound of classic crescent form (HU 484694, see section 10).

44 St Olaf's Church (Old Olnafirth Kirk), Voe, Shetland

Early 18th century AD.

HU 404636. On the N shore of Olna Firth just off the A 970.

Although roofless, the walls of this substantial rectangular church survive in good condition; it is built of harled rubble with freestone surrounds to the windows and arched doorways, and the iron fittings for external storm shutters can be seen on the window jambs. The most interesting feature is the burial aisle built as a projecting wing in the centre of the north side of the church; the upper storey, reached by an external stair, was used as a vestry and originally had access to an upper gallery within the church, and the ground floor was the burial aisle of the Giffords of Busta (see no. 18). An arched entrance in the north gable is embellished with an armorial panel above, bearing the arms of Thomas Gifford and Elizabeth Mitchell with their initials and the date of their marriage in 1714. Inside there is a fine graveslab set into the long wall on either side, each carved with the Gifford arms and the motto 'spare nought' above, and a long but now illegible inscription on the lower part of the slab.

To the north-west of the modern graveyard wall, there are traces of an earlier curvilinear enclosure, perhaps belonging to an earlier church.

St Olaf's Church, Voe (no. 44)

*St Olaf's Church, Voe:
Gifford burial aisle (no. 44)*

*St Olaf's Church, Voe: Gifford
armorial panel on graveslab
(no. 44)*

Lady Kirk, Pierowall, Westray (no. 45)

Lady Kirk, Pierowall: graveslabs (no. 45)

45 Lady Kirk, Pierowall, Westray, Orkney

17th century AD.
HY 439488. In Pierowall on the shore of the bay, 1 km SW of the pier.
HBM (SDD).

There are traces of the medieval fabric in the walls of this church, but most of the visible structure was built in the late 17th century—the date of 1674 is carved on the south skewput (the lowest stone at eaves level) of the east gable. The nave was re-aligned, somewhat wider than before, and the chancel was replaced by a laird's aisle, the whole structure distinctly canted. Within the laird's aisle are two 17th century tombstones with exceptionally fine lettering, one of which has the emblems of mortality carved in high relief and an effective chequered margin.

46 St Olaf's Church, Lunda Wick, Unst, Shetland

12th century AD and later.
HP 566040. Close to the SW shore of Lunda Wick, a walk of almost 1 km NW from Lund farm, some 5 km NW of Uyeasound.

Dedicated to St Olaf, the ruins of this simple rectangular church represent the sole example of the medieval churches of Unst to survive in recognisable form. It occupies a classic situation on the shores of a sheltered bay on the west coast of the island. The east end of the church has been rebuilt on the original foundations, but the rest dates from the 12th century and displays characteristically small windows and a doorway in the west gable with inclined jambs and a semi-circular arch. The church went out of use in the 18th century, but its earlier importance may still be gauged from two unusual 16th century tombstones preserved there. Inscribed in Low German, one commemorates Segelbad Detken in 1573 and the other Hinrick Segelcken in 1585, both men being Dutch merchants from Bremen.

47 St Ninian's Isle, Church, Shetland

12th–13th centuries AD.

HU 368208. South from Lerwick on the A 970 take the B 9122 SW towards Scousburgh; at HU 383200 take the signposted minor road off to the W; park and walk across to the island.

Excavations in the 1950s revealed the remains of a medieval church first built in the 12th century and enlarged in the 13th century into a church with a rectangular nave and possibly apsidal chancel; it is likely that this church had been abandoned and then demolished in the mid 18th century, after which its ruins had been entirely hidden by windblown sand until the excavation. The church had been built on the site of an earlier chapel with its accompanying graveyard, and it was in this earlier chapel that the famous silver treasure had been buried, beneath the nave of the medieval church: 28 silver objects had been buried for safe-keeping, together with part of the jawbone of a porpoise, in a wooden chest made of larch in a small pit beneath a stone slab, sometime around AD 800 (RMS; replicas in Shetland Museum, Lerwick). The slab was itself part of an earlier cross-slab, and the excavations produced an important collection of Early Christian stones, together with a hogback tombstone of 11th century date. Some of the stones represent components of finely decorated Early Christian stone shrines (Shetland Museum).

St Ninian's Isle today is accessible at virtually all times across a massive natural causeway of sand, and it is likely that, even at low tide, the island was accessible at low tide, a situation very similar to that of the Brough of Birsay in Orkney (no. 57). There was also evidence of prehistoric occupation beneath the later structures, at which date the island may have been more truly an island.

St Ninian's Isle, Shetland (no. 47)

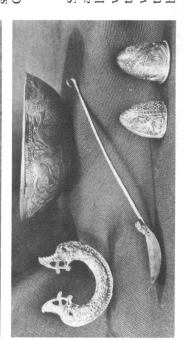

St Ninian's Isle church (no. 47)

St Ninian's Isle silver hoard: sword chape, bowl, spoon and cones

95

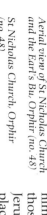

Aerial view of St Nicholas Church and the Earl's Bu, Orphir (no. 48)

St Nicholas Church, Orphir (no. 48)

48 St Nicholas Church, Orphir, Orkney

Early 12th century AD.

HY 334044. On the A 964 about 14.5 km from Kirkwall, take the minor road to Orphir; signposted.

HBM (SDD).

To visit Orphir is to be transported back into saga-times, for despite their fragmentary state the remains of these buildings neatly fit one of the few circumstantial descriptions in *Orkneyinga Saga*.

'There was a great drinking-hall at Orphir, with a door in the south wall near the eastern gable, and in front of the hall, just a few paces down from it, stood a fine church. On the left as you came into the hall was a large stone slab, with a lot of big ale vats behind it, and opposite the door was the living-room.'

In the early 12th century, Orphir was the seat of Earl Hakon Paulsson, who was responsible for the murder of Earl Magnus on Egilsay c 1117 but managed himself to die in his bed five years later. In between those events, he made a pilgrimage to Rome and to Jerusalem where, we are told, 'he visited the holy places and bathed in the River Jordan'. One of the places that he would have visited was the Church of the Holy Sepulchre, and this must have been the impetus to building a similar round church on his own estate at Orphir.

Only a third of the church survives but the rest of its plan is marked out on the ground: a precisely circular nave, 6.1 m in internal diameter, into which there would presumably have been an entrance at the west, with a semicircular apse on the east.

The church was complete until 1757, when it was largely demolished and its masonry used to build a new parish church alongside; ironically, the latter has now been demolished to reveal as much as possible of the earlier church. The apse is still intact with its half-barrel ceiling and internal plastering and a rounded-headed window above the seating for the altar, and early accounts of the nave describe its domed roof with a central hole to provide light.

A few metres away, or a few paces as the saga-writer put it, are the excavated walls of a large building, most probably the Earl's hall. Late Norse artefacts have been found in the vicinity, but more excavation is needed to establish the layout and extent of this important site.

49* St Magnus Cathedral, Kirkwall, Orkney
12th–15th centuries AD.
HY 449108. In the centre of the town.

The history of this remarkable cathedral goes back beyond the year in which its long programme of building began, 1137, to the year in which died the man to whom it was dedicated: Earl Magnus, who was murdered on Egilsay c 1117. His body was taken to Christ Church at Birsay and became a focus of pilgrimage—*Orkneyinga Saga* relates that 'a bright heavenly light was often seen over Magnus' grave' and that people were cured of illnesses by praying at his graveside. At first the church in Orkney was highly sceptical of the new cult growing up around Magnus, but eventually he was accepted as a saint and his bones became holy relics. Some time later, Bishop William was persuaded to transfer the relics to the church in Kirkwall, presumably to St Olaf's Church.

According to the saga, the impetus to build a new cathedral at Kirkwall came not from within the church but as a vow made by Earl Rognvald, then seeking control of the earldom: if he succeeded, he would build 'a stone minster at Kirkwall more magnificent than any in Orkney', which would be dedicated to St Magnus and would hold his relics. The episcopal seat was also to be in Kirkwall, and it has been suggested that Rognvald's vow reflects not only the medieval belief in the efficacy of saintly relics but also a shrewd political move on the part of the Orcadian Church, promising support for Rognvald in return for a fine cathedral and a new and more powerful centre for the bishopric. Rognvald succeeded in taking over the earldom and work began on building the Cathedral of St Magnus.

Its completion was to take far longer than anyone can have envisaged at the start, but its final splendour was well worth the delay—and indeed it was a magnificent structure at all intervening stages of the work, for the earliest part to be built was the choir, completed

St Magnus Cathedral, Kirkwall: west front (no. 49)

probably around 1142, which has been described as 'the finest Romanesque work north of Durham'. Comparison with both Durham and Dunfermline suggests that either Englishmen or Scotsmen were responsible for the design and execution of St Magnus Cathedral, a practice familiar from Norway itself at this period, when foreign expertise was often sought to build the great churches.

It appears that the foundations were laid at the start for the whole building, and work on the superstructure began at the east end of what was designed to be a cruciform Romanesque church with aisled choir and nave, projecting transepts and an apse at the east end. As work progressed, this design was modified and enlarged, and its style changed according to the fashion of the time—compare the piers of the nave, for instance: at the east end, the first pier on the north side and the first two on the south are in early 12th century Romanesque style with multicubical capitals and chamfered bases, whereas the next five piers on the north and four on the south are in late 12th century Transitional style with moulded capitals and bases. In the 13th century the building was enlarged by removing the apse at the east end and extending the aisled choir eastwards for another three bays. The three doorways at the west end of the cathedral were built at this time, enriched with carved decoration similar to that used in the choir, each with shafted jambs and pointed arches. Notice the use of alternate red and white stone in the arches, for this is one of the major and very pleasing decorative devices used inside the church as well, for instance as horizontal banding on the east wall of the south transept.

Prior to whitewashing in the 19th century, the interior was even more colourful, for it was painted with formal designs in red and black; unfortunately little traces of this survives, for both the whitewash and most of the underlying paintwork were removed in the late 19th century. Although the structure of the

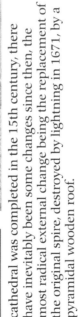

cathedral was completed in the 15th century, there have inevitably been some changes since then, the most radical external change being the replacement of the original spire, destroyed by lightning in 1671, by a pyramidal wooden roof.

There is a fine series of medieval and later tombstones in the Cathedral, including the Paplay tomb, a 14th century arched tomb recessed into the wall of the south aisle of the nave. Other sculptures include early 16th century effigies of St Magnus and the Norwegian King Olaf, as well as the burgh mercat cross. Three famous men of the 12th century were buried in the new minster: Bishop William, Earl Rognvald and, eventually, St Magnus himself. The bones of Bishop William were discovered in 1848 in a tomb in the

choir—he had apparently been moved from the original choir into the newly extended east end in the 13th century. Both having been canonised, the bones of St Rognvald and St Magnus would have been kept in resplendent caskets or reliquaries in the choir, until they were hidden for safety at the time of the Reformation. In each of the rectangular piers separating the 12th century choir from its 13th century extension, there is a cavity at a height of about 2.7 m; that in the north pier was discovered in 1848 and in it was a wooden box containing the loose bones of an incomplete male skeleton believed to be that of Rognvald, and a similar discovery in 1919 in the south pier contained the bones of St Magnus. The saga account of his death makes it clear that he died of a great blow on the head, and the skull in the casket showed unmistakeable signs of such a blow.

St Magnus Cathedral: tower and transept from south (no. 49)

St Magnus Cathedral: door in north side of nave (no. 49)

St Magnus Cathedral: piers in nave (no. 49)

St Magnus Church, Egilsay (no. 50)

50 St Magnus Church, Egilsay, Orkney

12th century AD.
HY 466303. The church stands on a knoll some 700 m E of the pier of the W side of the island; ferry from Tingwall.
HBM (SDD).

This is one of the finest of the early churches in the Northern Isles, dedicated to the earl who was murdered on the island c 1117, Magnus Erlendsson. It is thought to have replaced an earlier church in which Earl Magnus prayed before his death, and the spot where tradition believes the fatal blow to have been struck (HY 470300) is marked by a monument set up in 1937, the octocentenary of the foundation of St Magnus Cathedral.

Although roofless, the church is otherwise virtually complete, and its elegant tower still dominates the island. Built in Romanesque style, probably in the second quarter of the 12th century, it consists of a rectangular nave with a square-ended chancel at its east end and a round tower at its west end; the doorways and the original windows have rounded arches, and the chancel has a barrel-vaulted roof. There was an upper floor to the chancel, where the priest could lodge overnight. The north door to the nave and all the windows (including two later lintelled windows) have been blocked up since the church went out of use in the early 19th century, but it is possible to see the bar-hole on the east side of the south door to the nave, which held the bar to close the wooden door from the inside in times of trouble. At such times the tower could become an invaluable sanctuary, for it could be entered only from within the church; as well as the ground-floor door, a first-floor door gave access to an upper gallery in the nave, from which the priest's lodging over the chancel could also be reached. The tower survives to a height of 14.9 m but it was originally higher, perhaps almost 20 m high with four or five storeys, reached one from another by wooden ladders. The arrangement of windows in the tower is very ingenious: on the ground floor the window faces south, on the first floor it faces west, on the second east and on the third there are four windows, one to each quarter of the compass. A sketch of the church in 1822 shows flagstone roofs, including a conical roof to the tower, and the gables still retain their crowsteps.

51 St Mary's Chapel, Wyre, Orkney

12th century AD.
HY 443262. On the NW side of the island close to Cubbie Roo's Castle (no. 42); a walk of some 1.5 km from the jetty, by ferry from Tingwall. HBM (SDD).

This typical Romanesque chapel was built in the 12th century to serve the Christian Norse family whose hall or Bu is remembered in the name of the modern farm, the Bu of Wyre, and for whom Cubbie Roo's Castle (no. 42) was built. Although roofless, it is in good repair not only because it is in state care but also because it was partially restored in the late 19th century by General Traill Burroughs of Trumland House on Rousay.

Consisting of a rectangular nave and a square chancel, both chancel and nave are entered through semicircular arches, and traces of the original plaster may be seen on the inside walls and, beneath modern harling, on the exterior. A single window survives high in the south wall of the nave and another in the chancel.

Eynhallow church (no. 52)

52 Eynhallow Church, Orkney

12th century AD.
HY 359288. In the S part of the island: enquire of the Orkney Tourist Office about means of reaching the island. HBM (SDD).

The original identity of this most interesting group of buildings was entirely unsuspected until the mid 19th century. They had been in domestic use as houses since the 16th century until, in 1851, an epidemic of fever led to their evacuation; in order to make the buildings uninhabitable, the roofs were removed and in the process it was realised that part of the complex was an old church. The site was not properly cleared of debris until 1897, when the celebrated architect of Melsetter (no. 13), Professor W R Lethaby, was there to examine and report on the structure.

The name Eynhallow means Holy Isle from Old Norse *Eyin Helga*, which suggests that there may have been a small Celtic monastery here even before the 12th century church was built. Its monastic status at the latter period is implied by the story in *Orkneyinga Saga* (chap. 97) of the kidnapping of Olaf, the son of Svein Asleifarson of Gairsay and foster-son of Kolbein Hruga of Wyre; the kidnappers knew where to find Olaf on Eynhallow, and it is most likely that the boy was there to be educated in the monastery.

The church was built to a relatively sophisticated design: a rectangular nave opens at the east end into a rectangular chancel and at the west end into a substantial square porch (it is even possible that the latter represents the lower part of a tower). Although the walls both of the church and the adjacent buildings survive to roof-level, it is very difficult to analyse the architectural sequences present, because of additions and modifications relating to the domestic use of the site from the 16th century onwards, though the latter are interesting in themselves. The archaic, even primitive, character of various of the doorways

Eynhallow church: chancel and nave arches and west door (no. 52)

and archways of the church is unmistakeable and somewhat at variance with the grand layout. The west and north doorways into the porch are original and very narrow (0.46 m): the triangular arch of the west door is formed by two inclined slabs, while the round arch of the north door is cut into a single block of red freestone with a crude moulding on its external face. Entry into the nave is through a semi-circular arch of split slabs, while the arch between nave and chancel is a most ingenious rendering of the pointed arch that became fashionable in the 12th century. The springers and keystone are triangular blocks carved out of red freestone, allowing the rest of the arch to consist of the usual split slabs, a most economical way to achieve a pointed arch without mortar and with the minimum of dressed stone.

west, and originally belonged to an earlier church on the site. A fine church with twin towers, comparable to the single-towered St Magnus on Egilsay (no. 50), is known to have existed here and an Early Christian ancestry for the site is indicated by the recent find from nearby excavations of a fragment of a cross-incised grave-marker. These excavations have uncovered a Norse farm probably of the 10th and 11th centuries and an earlier Pictish settlement, and it is clear that Skaill has a long history of Dark Age, Viking and early medieval settlement against which its hogback monument may be set. In the 11th century, Skaill was the Orkney home of Thorkell, foster-father to Earl Thorfinn, and was undoubtedly a Christian Norse household.

53 Skaill, Hogback Tombstone, Deerness, Orkney

Late 11th–early 12th century AD.

HY 588063. At the termination of the A 960 from Kirkwall to Deerness, take the B 9050 to Skaill. The stone is inside the Session House attached to the modern church.

This is a well-preserved hogback of red sandstone, 1.73 m long, with four rows of *tegulae* or roof-tiles carved along either side, the tiles increasing in size towards the base. It was found in the north-east corner of the churchyard, lying east-north-east/west-south-

54 St Boniface Church, Hogback Tombstone, Papa Westray, Orkney

12th century AD.

HY 488527. In the graveyard on the E side of the church, approached by a track leading W from the road between Holland and North Hill.

This monument is contemporary with the early use of the adjacent ruined church, which has its origins in the 12th century. It lies in an east-west direction, accompanied by a small upright headstone, and it is carved from a block of red sandstone, 1.55 m long, with a deep groove running along its flat ridge and three rows of *tegulae* (roof-tiles) carved along each side.

8

VIKING-AGE MONUMENTS

The Scandinavian colonisation of the Northern Isles was arguably the single most formative event in their history since the initial human settlement of these islands, and yet there are remarkably few proven Viking-age monuments to be seen on the ground. The situation is even more noticeable elsewhere in Scotland and in the British Isles in general, where there are greater problems of locating sites of this period, let alone of preserving them—with the notable exception, of course, of the great trading centres of York and Dublin. In the Northern Isles, many sites are discovered through coastal erosion (with consequent problems for their preservation) and, for Orkney more than for Shetland, *Orkneyinga Saga* with its named farms and locations is an invaluable tool. Many more settlements and graves have been located and even excavated than remain as visible monuments, and there is a strong case for rectifying the balance by preserving and opening to the public the complex at Westness on Rousay in Orkney (HY 375294): here there are not only the domestic buildings of a settlement but, on the shore, a contemporary boat-naust in which the family longship could be sheltered over the winter, and the family cemetery in which an amazing variety of graves has been found, including a burial in a real timber boat and a skeuomorphic boat-grave built in stone, together with rich gravegoods. But none of these structures is visible above the surface of the ground, for without consolidation excavated sites must be backfilled in order to prevent collapse.

Late Norse monuments of the 12th century have been included in earlier sections of the book: St Magnus Cathedral, the various smaller churches and hogback tombstones and Cubbie Roo's Castle, for they are not part of the Viking-age proper. As in Scandinavia, it is normally considered that the Viking-age in the Northern Isles covers the period from about AD 800 to about AD 1050, although Scandinavian influence on the islands remained strong for several centuries later. The settlements on the Brough of Birsay (no. 57) and at Jarlshof (no. 55) span this period, and there are important traces of contemporary industrial activity at the Cunningsburgh steatite quarries (no. 56). Stones inscribed with the Scandinavian runic alphabet have been found in a number of places, including the Brough of Birsay and Cunningsburgh, but these have been gathered into museums; of those still in their original location, the marvellous collection of runes inscribed on the walls of Maes Howe neolithic chambered tomb (no. 95) and the brief inscription on one of the stones of the Ring of Brodgar (no. 83) have been described under the appropriate monuments later in the book.

Although there are few major Viking-age monuments in terms of surviving visible structure, it is impossible not to be aware, as one explores the islands, of the strength and impact of the Scandinavian colonisation, simply by absorbing placenames and their implications. As you wait for the ferry at Tingwall on

Aerial view of Jarlshof, Shetland (no. 55)

the east coast of Orkney mainland (HY 403228), think of all that the name implies; Old Norse *thingvollr* means parliament field, where leading Norsemen gathered to discuss legal business. Was it held here because this place was central between the great families of mainland and those of the islands? Another Tingwall in Shetland, in the hinterland beyond Lerwick, has a Loch of Tingwall where, at the northern end, there is a promontory known as Law Ting Holm (HU 418434); this was once a tiny islet connected to the shore by a narrow causeway, which can still be seen in the boggy ground—surely a safe and strategic place for warring family leaders to meet.

Given the special importance of the sea as a means of transport and communication to the Vikings, it is not surprising that most of their settlements are located close to the coast and close to good landing places for boats. In Orkney, the Bay of Birsay, the Bays of Swandro and Westness on Rousay, Sandside Bay at Skaill in Deerness, the Bays of Pierowall and Tuquoy on Westray are all confirmed by excavations to have been foci of Norse settlement; in Shetland, there have been fewer excavations, but the West Voe of Sumburgh and, on Unst, Lunda Wick and Sand Wick are proven foci of settlement, and there are many other ideal locations begging exploration. The delapidated remains of an excavated Norse house may be seen on the slope above Lunda Wick at Underhoull (HP 573043).

The pattern of settlement during the Viking-age was essentially one of scattered farmsteads rather than villages, though the presence of a large cemetery of pagan graves excavated in the 19th century at Pierowall on Westray may suggest that a small hamlet existed there. The typical farm of the 9th and 10th centuries consisted of an oblong dwelling house, known as a hall-house, with separate out-buildings which might include a byre, a stable, a threshing barn and other storehouses, and even a bath-house. If the farm were occupied over several centuries, as at Jarlshof (no. 55), it is possible to trace the inevitable modifications and rebuildings that took place, and to see that, by the end of the 11th century, the true longhouse was becoming fashionable, with the addition to one end of the dwelling-house of a byre. In late Norse times from the 12th century onwards, houses became more complex in design with extra rooms and porches attached to their long walls.

It is very noticeable that Viking-age farms were often built literally on top of the ruins of earlier native sites, perhaps as a lazy way of getting building-stone or perhaps out of inbred habit, good land being at such a premium along the fjords of their west Norwegian homelands that it was normal to rebuild on exactly the same spot. The habit was taken to absurd lengths at Saevar Howe in Birsay, Orkney (HY 245269), where in the 9th century Norsemen built houses perched on top of a huge, tell-like mound that contained the ruins of Pictish and earlier buildings; the ruined Norse buildings were in their turn capped by a cemetery of long cist graves (stone-lined graves) in the 10th century.

The economic basis of such farms differed little from that of later times, or indeed from that of the existing native population of the islands: cattle, sheep and pigs were reared, and the sea was exploited both for fish and for shellfish to use as fish-bait. Cereal crops were cultivated, including bere (barley) and oats, and sometimes flax was grown so that linen cloth could be made. On the face of it, a normal farming life, essentially self-sufficient apart from some bartered goods such as soapstone, cooking vessels or metal tools and jewellery—but there was another side to Viking life, one which continued even into the 12th century. This was raiding, the true viking expeditions for adventure and plunder. *Orkneyinga Saga* describes how one such farmer-viking lived, Svein Asleifarson: 'Winter he would spend at home on

Gairsay, where he entertained some eighty men at his own expense. His drinking hall was so big, there was nothing in Orkney to compare with it. In the spring he had more than enough to occupy him with a great deal of seed to sow which he saw to carefully himself. Then when that job was done, he would go off plundering in the Hebrides and in Ireland on what he called his 'spring trip', then back home just after mid-summer, where he stayed till the cornfields had been reaped and the grain was safely in. After that he would go off raiding again, and never came back till the first month of winter was ended. This he used to call his 'autumn -trip''. Such expeditions added all sorts of exotic goods to Norse homes, for merchant ships carrying fine cloth, wine and other imports were as much targets for attack as houses on land.

Nor should the extensive foreign travels of many Norsemen be forgotten as a source of exotic goods and ideas; they went on pilgrimages to Rome and beyond and on crusades to the Holy Land in the 11th and 12th centuries, as the round church at Orphir (no. 48) recalls with its design copying that of the church of the Holy Sepulchre in Jerusalem, and there was constant traffic between the far-flung Atlantic colonies. A runic inscription in Tankerness House Museum, which is likely originally to have come from the 12th century church at Orphir, has been shown to contain a very special form of the r-rune, unknown outside Greenland apart from this example and another from Trondheim in Norway–this would seem to imply the presence in Orkney of a Norseman from one of the Greenland settlements.

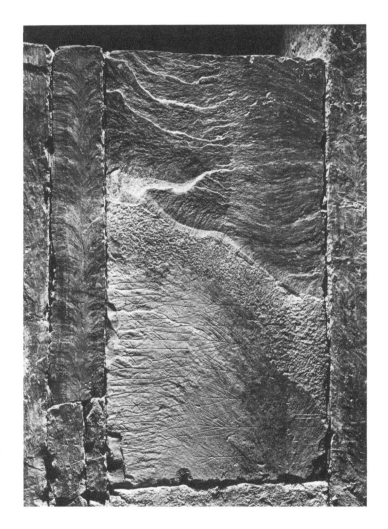

Runic inscription in Maes Howe, Orkney (no. 95)

Jarlshof: Viking-age settlement (no. 55)

55* Jarlshof, Shetland

Medieval, Viking-age and prehistoric.
HU 398095. At the S tip of the Shetland mainland, near Sumburgh Hotel, S from the A 970.
HBM (SDD).

The multi-period site at Jarlshof is physically dominated by the ruined 17th century laird's house (no. 24), but it is best known for its extensive Viking-age settlement, first discovered in 1933 and thus demonstrating Sir Walter Scott's percipience in inventing the name 'Jarlshof'. The proper name is Sumburgh, which derives from an Old Norse name, but it is impossible to know whether it was used in Viking times for this particular farm, for the whole headland or indeed for another Norse site as yet undiscovered in the area. The earliest recorded form of the name is *Svinaborg* in 15th century documents, which may mean either 'Svein's fort' or 'fort of pigs'; if the latter, perhaps it was a derogatory term derived by the Norsemen from the ruins of the old broch, which must still have been quite impressive in Viking times. Although Sumburgh Head is mentioned in *Orkneyinga Saga*, there is no hint of an important farm nearby, which suggests that, despite its prominence in the surviving archaeological record, Jarlshof may have been a place of little consequence in its own day.

The remains of the Norse buildings form such a complex tangle of superimposed walls that it can be quite difficult for the visitor to sort them out; the best place to start is with the earliest dwelling-house, House 1, the floor-area of which can easily be distinguished by its modern covering of white gravel. This was first built in the 9th century as a typical hall-house, some 21 m long, with a long open hearth in the centre of the hall, a row of timber posts down each long side to help support the roof, and low benches lining the walls; subsequent modifications added cross-walls and elongated the building, particularly by the addition of a byre at the east end, entered by a long paved passage-way. Outhouses belonging to the early hall-house included a possible bath-house outside the west end of the main building, which is visible as a small square structure with a central hearth. Most of the later Norse houses were built at right angles and to the north and west of House 1, each of them undergoing later modifications of design, and the entire complex is thought to date from the 9th to the 13th or 14th centuries to judge from datable objects found either in the buildings or in middens outside them.

The succeeding medieval farm built probably in the early 14th century is a rare early example of the sort of farm still being built into recent times (see section 5). It consisted of a dwelling-house and barn built parallel

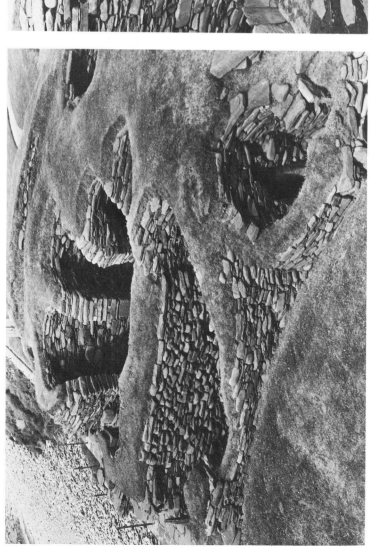

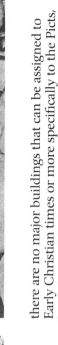

Jarlshof, wheelhouse north-west of broch (no. 55)

Jarlshof, interior of wheelhouse showing piers and central hearth (no. 55)

and close to each other, with a small circular corn-drying kiln set into one corner of the barn (only the northern parts of the two buildings now survive, the rest having been removed in order to expose prehistoric structures beneath). The farm seems to have been inhabited during both the 14th and 15th centuries.

The archaeological importance of Viking-age Jarlshof tends to overshadow the earlier remains on the site, but these too are of considerable interest, both as individual buildings and as a sequence showing the development of a settlement that appears to have been continuous over some 2,500 years prior to the arrival of the Norsemen. Among the excavated structures,

there are no major buildings that can be assigned to Early Christian times or more specifically to the Picts, but it is possible that our understanding of this period of the site's history is grossly incomplete: such buildings may lie undetected in unexcavated areas (such as under the 16th century house) or they may have been destroyed by coastal erosion.

The two wheelhouses on the north side of the broch are particularly interesting and well-preserved examples of a distinctive type of dwelling that was built in the Western Isles of Scotland as well as the Northern Isles during the early centuries of the first millennium AD. This was a circular stone-built house in which radial piers not only divided up the internal

perimeter of the house into storage and sleeping areas but also helped to support the roof—presumably a conical roof with a timber frame and turf or thatch covering. The hearth would be in the centre of the house. Partly overlain by the smaller wheelhouse are the remains of an earlier prototype, in which there is a gap between the piers and the house-wall. Less complete remains of wheelhouses survive both within and on the south-east side of the broch. The wheelhouse was a substantial and, at Jarlshof, a most beautifully designed and constructed house, the equivalent in stone of the huge timber house with its internal ring of wooden posts to be found in southern Scotland and beyond in late prehistoric times. Only half of the broch survives, the rest having been lost into the sea, but the remains of two cells can be seen built into the thickness of the massively solid broch wall.

In front of the small museum are the earliest prehistoric houses, a series of circular and oval buildings spanning much of the first and second

millennia BC, the later of which have attached underground storerooms or earth-houses. The best preserved of the earliest among them is Dwelling III, an oval house divided internally into small cells in the tradition seen elsewhere in Shetland, eg Pettigarths Field, Whalsay (no. 75). It was within the ruined walls of this house that an itinerant bronzesmith from Ireland set up his workshop around 800 BC, supplying the inhabitants with bronze swords and axes and other goods; many fragments of broken clay moulds were found, as well as structural traces of the smithy.

At the eastern-most corner of the site, adjacent to the medieval farm, are a few lengths of walling representing an oval house belonging to the very earliest occupation: abundant finds show links with late neolithic domestic sites in Orkney, especially with Skara Brae (no. 72). As with all the early prehistoric levels on this site, it is likely that only a fraction of the original settlement has been excavated, more lying hidden beneath later structures.

are covered with chisel marks. The method used in manufacturing steatite vessels was to carve out the rough shape of the bottom and sides of the vessel as if it were upside down on the rock, to detach this blank and to finish shaping its exterior and hollowing out the inside. The talcose rock is relatively easy to carve, being quite a soft stone that is soapy to the touch, hence its other name, soapstone, and it was used for a great number of purposes from early prehistoric times onwards.

Excavations at Jarlshof (no. 55), some 24 km to the south, produced a variety of steatite vessels that can be matched by the blanks and discarded waste in the quarries, and steatite grit used to strengthen the clay for pottery vessels demonstrates that steatite was being exploited by the beginning of the second millennium BC. Steatite was being used most extensively in the Viking-age and early medieval times, when round, oval and square vessels were in fashion consecutively from the 9th to 13th centuries, as well as steatite line-sinkers for fishing, spindle whorls, beads and lamps (small oval dishes with a hole at either end so that they could be suspended, the wick immersed in oil). At this period the industry must have been organised on a mass market, commercial scale, with its products being exported not only all over Shetland but also to Orkney and Iceland, which lack any source of steatite.

Steatite outcrops elsewhere in Shetland as well, and there are traces of ancient quarries both on Fetlar and on Unst, particularly at Clibberswick on Unst (HP 651121) where near vertical cliff-faces were somehow worked in what must have been terrifying conditions. Steatite was also very extensively exploited in Norway itself, and work is currently underway to establish methods of petrological analysis which will allow the origin of steatite artefacts to be identified more precisely than is possible at the moment—variety in the composition of the rock within a single deposit makes recognition of an object from one particular quarry very difficult.

56 Catpund Steatite Quarries, Cunningsburgh, Shetland

Early medieval, Viking-age and prehistoric.
HU 423270. Signposted A 970 from Lerwick to Sumburgh, about 19 km S of Lerwick.

The steatite quarries cover a very large area, almost 1 km long, from the shore below and to the east of the main road, rising on either side of the Catpund Burn to its headwaters in the hills to the west, but the best area to visit is immediately west of the road, involving a five to ten minute climb up beside the burn. Traces of quarrying can be seen both in the bed of the burn and on the rock outcrops on either side: most obvious are the projecting blanks for vessels that were never removed and the round and rectangular depressions where such blanks were removed, and the rock faces

Working faces in the bed of the Catpund Burn, Cunningsburgh (no. 56)

Brough of Birsay, Orkney (no. 57), with the incoming tide beginning to isolate the island

57* Brough of Birsay, Orkney

8th–12th centuries AD.

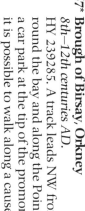
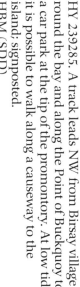

HY 239285. A track leads NW from Birsay village round the bay and along the Point of Buckquoy to a car park at the tip of the promontory. At low tide it is possible to walk along a causeway to the island; signposted. HBM (SDD).

To see the Brough of Birsay in summer is to appreciate its attraction for settlement: as a tidal island it is defensible and yet not isolated, and it is situated so as to enjoy all the advantages of this favoured corner of Orkney with its fertile land and sheltered landing places. The island is about 21 hectares in extent, sloping up from about 4 m OD on its east side to the sheer western cliffs, some 45 m high, where puffins live. The gentle slope facing mainland belies the incredible force of the Atlantic waves that break against its western face, for in winter the sea-spray rises so high that the entire island is washed by salt water; in Viking times, however, the climate was appreciably better than now, with an average mean temperature about 2°C higher, an enormous boon to the arable farmer and a calming influence on the winter storms.

Although the Brough was undoubtedly already a tidal island by late prehistoric times, there has been appalling coastal erosion over the last eight centuries, and much structural evidence of settlement has been lost into the sea, not only adjacent to the central area of buildings east of the church, where house walls and the boat slipway stop abruptly at the cliff edge, but also along the coast on either side. Recent excavations have concentrated on recording what is left of Viking-age and Pictish buildings along the cliff-edge and on the slice of land that will one day collapse into the sea, known as the Peerie Brough, the little Brough. This means that what has survived as a substantial archaeological site was originally considerably more extensive.

In Norse times, from around AD 800 until the 12th century or perhaps a little later, there was a major settlement here which must always have possessed a rather different status and character from the normal farm— if only because normal farming was impossible on the tiny island itself and must have been supplemented by the produce of fields and pastures on the adjacent mainland. It is possible that the home farm during the 9th century was the site which has been excavated but which is no longer visible on the Point of Buckquoy, where a dwelling-house, barn-byre and threshing barn were discovered. Cattle, sheep and pigs were reared on the Buckquoy farm, whereas the animal bones from excavations on the Brough suggest very logically that sheep were probably grazed on the island itself and beef was brought over ready slaughtered as joints.

The visible buildings are dominated by the church, a fine Romanesque creation which was probably built in the early 12th century; it is very small (the nave is only

Brough of Birsay: church and 12th century domestic buildings (no. 57)

Brough of Birsay: 12th century buildings east of the church (no. 57)

8.5 m by 5.8 m internally) but its design is quite sophisticated, with a square chancel and a semi-circular apse at the east end and traces of a probable square tower at the west end. There are semi-circular recesses for altars in the nave, on either side of the chancel arch, and the main altar, which was originally in the apse, is now in the chancel, whence it was moved in later medieval times when the church was a place of pilgrimage (the altar has also been restored in modern times). The proportions of the church and the warm colour of the sandstone are very pleasing—and the stone bench lining the north, south and west walls of the nave gives an excellent impression of its internal lay-out in the days before wooden pews.

To the north of the church are three ranges of buildings which, with the church on its fourth side, enclose a courtyard. This is thought by some scholars to have formed the kernel of a Benedictine monastery,

although unfortunately there is no documentary evidence to identify with certainty either its monastic status or the order to which the monastery belonged. The foundation of this early medieval church represents a return to an ecclesiastical status, for the site had an Early Christian chapel in pre-Norse times, but during the intervening 300 years the settlement is likely to have been purely secular.

At one time the church was thought to be the Christchurch built by Earl Thorfinn after his pilgrimage to Rome around 1050 and the buildings to the north of the church to be the Bishop's Palace of the earliest bishops of the Northern Isles, but it is now agreed that the church was built more than half a century later and that Christchurch and the seat of the bishopric were on the mainland beneath the modern village of Birsay (see no. 39).

113

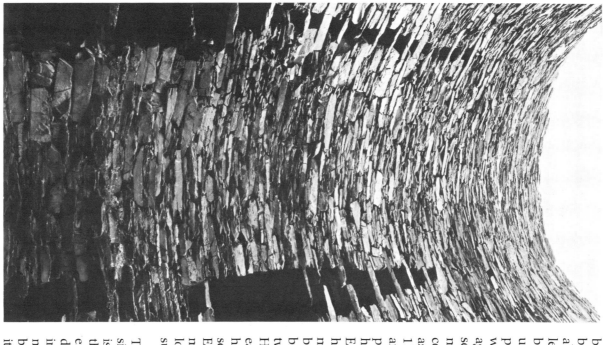

beautifully built, but so were those of many another broch; the answer must be, at least in part, that it was abandoned intact, that for some reason there was no lengthy period of occupation on the site after the broch-tower was no longer necessary; when it could be used as a quarry for stone to build lesser structures. Or perhaps the tower remained intact simply because it was such a grand achievement and might be needed again—as it was some nine centuries later. The broch seems to have been well known to the Norsemen and must even then have been in excellent and usable condition, for it is mentioned twice in Icelandic sagas as *Moseyjarborg*. Best recorded is the occasion in AD 1153 when, as *Orkneyinga Saga* relates, Earl Harald arrived at *Moseyjarborg* with his men, in furious pursuit of his mother's suitor. Erlend; as Harald had rejected Erlend's proposal to marry Margaret, Erlend had abducted the lady from Orkney and taken her to the broch at Mousa 'where everything had been made ready'. Earl Harald's forces surrounded the broch, cutting off all supplies, but they found that the broch was 'not an easy place to attack'. Sensibly the two sides negotiated. Erlend promised his support to Harald, who was still trying to win control over the earldom (this was just a year after Harald and his men had had a bad experience sheltering in Maes Howe, see no. 95), and there was a reconciliation, allowing Erlend and Margaret to marry. While the old broch might not be the most comfortable or romantic of love-nests, it was clearly still an impregnable refuge, susceptible only to a long-sustained siege.

The broch stands on a low rocky headland on the west side of the island of Mousa; on the mainland opposite is the broch of Burraland (HU 446231), and the pair of them seem to loom like sentinels over the southern entry into Mousa Sound. Neither has been excavated, despite the fact that Mousa has twice been cleared out in recent times (1861 and 1919). Traces of a rampart may still be seen on the landward side of Mousa broch, and there are records of a few outbuildings, but it is clear that the broch was never the focus of a

Broch of Mousa, Shetland (no. 64)

Skara Brae, Orkney (no. 72)

Midhowe Broch, Rousay (no. 60)

Knap of Howar, Papa Westray
(no. 73)

Ring of Brodgar, Orkney (no. 83)

Busta standing stone, Shetland
(no. 88)

how the hollow wall of the broch was built. At the top, there is now a safety grill across the interior of the broch, but it is thought that originally the tower would be open down to the roof of the timber gallery, with the wall-top taking the form of a parapet.

The island is now uninhabited, apart from sheep and ponies, but the ruin of the old Haa, a plain two-storey house, stands on the slope to the south-east of the broch, and the shell of a clack mill may be seen on the burn to the north-east. Sand Lodge, where the ferry leaves for Mousa, has some interesting features: at the north-west corner of the wall surrounded house of Sand Lodge, there is a well-kept dovecote, square with a pyramidal roof (HU 437248). There were copper mines in the vicinity in the early 19th century, and the masonry jetty and three surviving winches for hauling boats on to the shore represent 19th century fishery and boat-building activities.

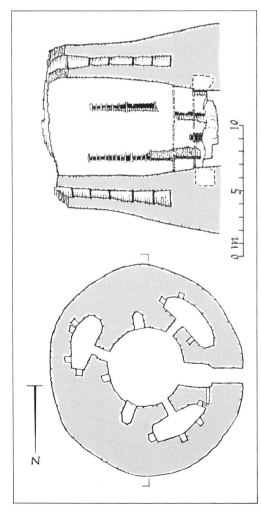

Plan and section of Broch of Mousa (no. 64)

village. At a height of just over 13 m, the tower must be almost complete, lacking perhaps another metre above the present wall-head; its diameter is about 15 m at the base, tapering elegantly to about 12 m at the top. The solid base of the wall is immensely thick, so that the entrance passage is very long and the interior only 6 m across. There are no guard-cells opening off the passage, but there are three large cells within the wall entered originally from the broch interior just above ground-level, though their entrances are now on a level with later structures built inside the tower—indeed the layout of the interior is almost entirely secondary to the broch, and represents a wheelhouse inserted in perhaps the 3rd or 4th century AD.

Two ledges projecting from the internal wall-face of the tower represent the floor and roof heights of an original timber gallery, at which level, reached now by a stone stair but perhaps originally by a ladder, there is an entrance leading to the stairway inside the broch-wall. It is still possible to climb this stair up to the top of the tower, and it is an experience that not only gives some impression of what it must have been like to live in such a broch but also allows a fuller appreciation of

65 Castle of Burwick, Fort, South Ronaldsay, Orkney

Late 1st millennium BC.
ND 434842. Follow the A 961 from Kirkwall to its very end at Burwick, and walk W for 0.5 km to the coast.

The Castle of Burwick is almost an island, for it is joined to the mainland only by a very narrow neck of land, although this may have been somewhat wider in iron-age times, and the cliffs are high and sheer. Three lines of rampart with ditches between them have been built on mainland to guard access to the Castle, and a fourth rampart lies across the approach on the Castle side; in the long grass within the forts, there are traces of structures, presumably houses, beneath the turf.

Preserved within St Mary's Church at Burwick is a stone carved with a pair of footprints, similar to that at Clickhimin (no. 61), but its original provenance is unknown.

Aerial view of Ness of Burgi fort, Shetland (no. 66)

66 Ness of Burgi, Fort, Shetland

Late 1st millennium BC.
HU 388083. About 1.5 km before the A 970 terminates at Grutness pier near Sumburgh Airport, a minor road leads S along the Scatness peninsula; from the end of the road, it is a walk of just over 1 km to the fort.
HBM (SDD).

The walk to Ness of Burgi is something of an adventure trail, for the headland is very rocky and precipitous and must be reached by clambering over the remains of a very narrow arch of bare and jagged rocks; even to view it from a safe distance conveys a strong impression of the desperate lengths to which iron-age people were prepared to go to achieve ultimate defence (allowing for erosion over the past 2000 years, this must still have been a daunting place to live). In many ways, it was ideal, for there was

grazing and cultivable land on the main Scatness peninsula to the north, and the attraction of the area is underlined by the presence of another, presumably contemporary, fort on the next headland to the north, known as Scatness East (HU 388087). Both are examples of a highly specialised type of fort, characterised by the addition of a stone blockhouse.

Once across the storm-beach and on to the headland, there is a low outer rampart with an entrance on the east, where it would be visible from the main fort, and then an area of open ground in front of the latter. The stones from the excavation and consolidation of the site have been piled neatly into a low rectangular mound that looks persuasively authentic but is entirely modern, including the cist-like chamber built amongst the stones. The headland on which the fort stands has suffered much erosion and the area enclosed, now very restricted, would originally have been considerably more viable in terms of living space.

The neck of the headland is spanned by two rock-cut ditches on either side of a massive rampart, once faced with stone, with a central entrance aligned with the blockhouse entrance. Although the south-west end of the blockhouse has been destroyed by erosion, the rest is in good condition and survives to the height (about 1.2 m) of the lintel-slabs roofing the passage, of which several remain in position. The entrance passage retains the checks against which the door would be closed and the bar-holes on either side into which the holding bar could be drawn; in both cases, the bar-hole extends into a mural cell, that to the north entered from the passage and that to the south entered from the fort interior. A third, largely restored, cell survives on the south, apparently entered from the end of the blockhouse as at Clickhimin. The cells would originally have had corbelled and lintelled roofs and lintelled passages, and the blockhouse probably rose to a height of some 2.5 m to 3 m. Nothing is known of the interior of the fort, but there would presumably have been domestic buildings.

and the defences are best seen from the mainland: traces survive of four lines of earthen and stone defence, the outermost now just a line of boulders but the next retaining a good wall-face built of rounded stones. Inside the fort, there are oval house-foundations visible as hollows in the turf along the eroded west side.

67 Ness of Garth, Fort, Shetland
Late 1st millennium BC.
HU 216582. About 2 km before the A 971 from Bridge of Walls terminates at Melby pier, take a minor road E to Crawton, and walk N down a track beside a small loch to the shore at Ness.

There is clearly ferocious erosion along this exposed Atlantic coast, and the promontory on which the fort was built is not only now reduced in area but also separated from the mainland (though cut off only by high tides). This is a multi-ramparted promontory fort

Ness of Garth fort, Shetland, from the air (no. 67)

The remains of two clack mills, one with millstones and stone-lined lade intact, may be seen on the way to the fort, and, at the head of the track close to the public road, there is an excellent example of a crescentic burnt mound (HU 214577), a type of monument described in the next chapter. On the way back from Sandness along the A 971, pause on the hill above Burga Water on your left to admire the small stone fort or dun on its tiny island in the loch (HU 234539).

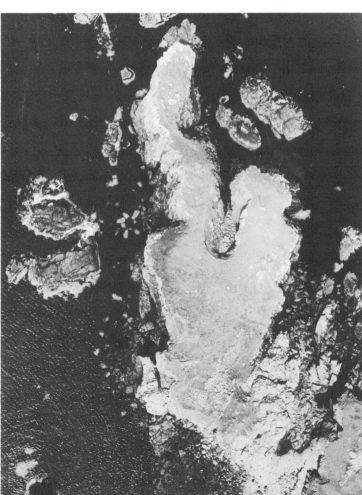

68 Brough of Stoal, Fort, Yell, Shetland
Late 1st millennium BC.
HU 545873. On the A 968, some 7 km N of Burravoe, on the E side of the island, take the minor road at Otterwick NE to Aywick, along the coast to the NE.

This dramatic coastline, from which there is a marvellous view across Colgrave Sound to Fetlar, is indented with deep and sheer geos, two of which flank the eroded promontory on which the fort stands. There are three impressively well-preserved ramparts, each over 2m high, with ditches between them; the original entrance causeway must have been to one side and now destroyed. There are traces of internal structures, which could conceivably be the remains of a broch which has partly toppled into the sea but which may represent some less grandiose building. The situation and the defences are certainly very similar to those at the Broch of Burland on southern mainland (HU 445360), a spectacular but very dangerous site at which the broch is now so close to the precipice that it may one day disappear.

Grain earth-house, Kirkwall: entrance passage (no. 69)

Grain earth-house: chamber (no. 69)

69* Grain, Earth-house, Kirkwall, Orkney

1st millennium BC.

HY 441116. In an industrial estate on the NW outskirts of Kirkwall, approached by a minor road leading E off the A 965 just beyond the causeway between the harbour and the Peerie Sea; signposted.

HBM (SDD).

This earth-house has remained in excellent condition, probably because it was constructed so deeply underground—some 2 m of earth separates its roof from the ground-surface, and a flight of steps leads down into the passage (the upper part of the stair is modern but the lower part is original). The passage curves in a gentle arc, lined with drystone walling and

roofed by flat lintels at a height of about 0.9 m, so that it is impossible to walk upright, but it opens into a well-built oval chamber which is just high enough, at 1.6 m, for most people to move about upright or almost upright. As a cellar for storing food supplies, comfort was not an important factor. The flat lintelled roof is supported on four free-standing pillars of stone.

When it was discovered in the 19th century, the earth-house was empty, but clear evidence was found of there having been a domestic settlement at ground-level: the basal courses of walls and a large pit full of ash, burnt wood, animal bones and shells. In 1982 a second smaller earth-house was discovered about 6 m to the west, which presumably belonged to the same settlement, but this is no longer visible.

70 Rennibister, Earth-house, Orkney

1st millennium BC.

HY 397125. Some 6.5 km WNW of Kirkwall on the A 965, signposted with car park; the earth-house is in the yard of a working farm, and cars should not be taken into the farmyard. HBM (SDD).

An interesting example of a modern farm on exactly the same spot as an iron-age farm, Rennibister lies close to the shore with access to a fertile area of land which has attracted settlement since neolithic times as demonstrated by three chambered cairns (nos 90, 100). Another earth-house was found in the 19th century near Saverock, between Rennibister and Grain. The presence of the earth-house at Rennibister was unsuspected until 1926 when its roof gave way beneath the weight of a threshing-machine passing

overhead, and a modern hatch and ladder now allow entry through the roof into the chamber. Original access was down the narrow lintelled passage opening into the opposite end of the chamber, though with a width and height of only about 0.7 m, it can never have been easy. The chamber is oval, its originally corbelled roof supported on four free-standing stone pillars, and its walls are furnished with five small recesses, one divided by a stone shelf. When it was first discovered, the end of the passage was filled with shells and domestic refuse, and a jumbled mass of human bones on the floor of the chamber proved to be the remains of six adults and twelve children. The fact that the skeletons were disarticulated implies that it was as bones rather than bodies that they were placed in the earth-house, presumably having originally been buried elsewhere, but it is not known why, or when, this was done.

Rennibister earth-house: chamber and entrance passage (no. 70)

10

EARLY PREHISTORIC MONUMENTS

One of the great joys of visiting the Northern Isles must be the insight into early prehistoric times offered by a variety of outstandingly well-preserved monuments that have somehow survived fifty or more centuries of human impact on their environment. Where else in north-west Europe can you hope to find the houses of people who lived and toiled 5000 years ago still standing to eaves level? Neolithic houses are rarely encountered above ground-level in the rest of the British Isles, and excavation yields few details of their interiors to match the stone-built furniture of Skara Brae—and it was surely by choice rather than necessity that stone was used, for there was plenty of driftwood available. The great standing stones, long known through the drawings and writing of early travellers from the 18th century onwards—Sir Walter Scott staged the final scenes of his novel *The Pirate* at the Stones of Stenness—and the discovery of Skara Brae has inspired many a poet and storyteller of the 20th century.

Burnt Mounds

Judged by quantity alone, burnt mounds would be the single most important class of prehistoric monument in the Northern Isles, for over 400 are known to exist or to have existed in the past, and yet little attention was paid to them until the 1970s when three were fully excavated. Before excavation, burnt mounds appear literally as mounds of burnt and shattered stone, grass-grown but often with burnt stones visible here and there, and they are always located near a source of freshwater; in size they vary from a few metres across to the largest known example, at Vaasetter on Fair Isle, which is 37 m by 27 m and 3 m high, and they are often crescentic in shape—classic examples are mentioned under no. 67 at Crawton in Shetland and in the Papa Westray excursion at Backiskaill, and good examples in the vicinity of other monuments detailed here are Fan Knowe near Dounby in Orkney (HY 299197) and Burnside near Hillswick in Shetland (HU 280784). At the latter site, the side-slabs of a stone trough can be seen within the crescent of the mound, and such troughs have frequently been encountered elsewhere, but the extent of the buried structures became apparent with excavations at Ness of Sound in Shetland and Beaquoy and Liddle in Orkney (Liddle, no. 71, is still visible).

Burnt mounds are in fact cooking places, where stones were heated on a hearth and thrown into troughs of water so as to boil the water for cooking large joints of meat; the stones, burnt and cracked, were then discarded in an arc round the cooking area. Cooking was carried out in oval stone-built shelters, which may have been communal cook-houses serving people living close by, and scientific dating of burnt stone and pottery has shown that they were used between about 1000 and 400 BC. Finds of agricultural tools and cereal

Skaill Bay and the neolithic village of Skara Brae (no. 72)

pollen, together with their distribution on good fertile soil, combine to demonstrate that burnt mounds belonged to farming communities. Very similar mounds occur elsewhere in the British Isles, particularly in Wales and Southern Ireland, but they are rare in Scotland outside the Northern Isles, where they occur even on the remote island of Foula.

Although roasting would seem the simplest method of cooking meat, there is no doubt that boiling was a popular alternative and, amongst people whose pottery was not strong enough to use over the fire and who lacked metal containers, boiling in a stone or wooden trough was acceptably efficient—it had an important advantage over roasting in that the melting fat was not lost into the fire. There is evidence of this type of cooking in early Irish literature and, closer to home, in a description of the Hebrides in the mid 18th century: 'the meaner sort of people still retain the custom of boiling their beef in the hide; or otherwise (being destitute of vessels of metal or earth) they put water into a block of wood made hollow by the help of the dirk and burning; and then with pretty large stones heated red-hot and successively quenched in that vessel, they keep the water boiling, till they have dressed their food.'

Settlements

The archaeological record leaves a distinct impression of material poverty among communities in the Northern Isles during the later 2nd and early 1st millennia BC, and, aside from the prolific burnt mounds, relatively few traces of domestic settlements have been found. A combination of climatic deterioration, bringing with it an increase in the formation of peat and barren moorland, and the effect of intense cultivation in late neolithic times seem to have led to short-term settlement and somewhat insubstantial buildings easily obliterated by later

ploughing. In some marginal areas traces survive of field-systems, clearance cairns (piles of stones cleared from the fields) and hut-circles of probable bronze-age date, but it takes a trained eye to distinguish them on the ground.

In contrast, the substantial settlements and tombs of the earlier 2nd millennium, 3rd and early 4th millennium reflect an era of economic stability and long-lasting farms, when a milder climate even allowed the cultivation of wheat, and there was the labour and the incentive to build on a grand scale. Skara Brae (no. 72) and Knap of Howar (no. 73) are remarkable both for their preservation and for the wealth of information afforded by their excavation, while the less well-preserved but no less interesting neolithic houses of Shetland astound by their very number. It is not difficult to envisage cereal cultivation in the modern contexts of the Orkney sites, but many of the Shetland houses are set in bleak moorland or half-submerged in peat, and yet there too, more than 4000 years ago, agriculture was as viable a part of the economy as rearing cattle and sheep or fishing. Traces of plough-furrows have been found at Links of Noltland on Westray, an important settlement hidden beneath the sand-dunes.

The dense concentration of settlements, field-systems, chambered tombs and cairns in the area around Gruting Voe in west mainland Shetland offers a rare and exciting opportunity to appreciate the early prehistoric landscape and to gain some impression of the numbers of people living in these remote northern islands. Without excavation, it is impossible to judge how many sites were in use at the same time, but, even so, radiocarbon dates from the few excavated early settlements have demonstrated that each is likely to have been inhabited over a very long period of seven or eight centuries, and the use of an individual tomb was equally long or even longer.

with thick stone slabs forming the sides and bottom of a watertight box, 1.6 m by 1.0 m and 0.6 m deep. When this trough was first excavated, it was half-full of burnt stones left from the last cooking. The eastern part of the shelter had been disturbed by recent quarrying for road-metal, but sufficient remained of the hearth to show that it had been set in an alcove in the wall and that the fuel used was peat. The position of the hearth suggests that the building was not roofed, for even if the alcove were itself roofed by lintels or corbelling, the danger of setting the rafters alight would be considerable; given the steam that must have been produced by the trough, an enclosed building would have been unbearable to work in, steam and smoke combining to make it impossible either to see or to breathe.

71 Liddle, Burnt Mound, South Ronaldsay, Orkney

Early 1st millennium BC.

ND 464841. Just before the A 961 terminates at Burwick,the B 9041 leads E; after 1.5 km, take the minor road S to Liddle farm, signposted; c 400 m NE of farmhouse.

This was formerly a very large burnt mound, about 2 m high, which had accumulated round an oval building on a slope above a small burn. The basal courses of the shelter survive to a height of almost a metre, the floor is paved and round the walls is a series of compartments formed by upright slabs, but the major feature is the sunken trough, massively built

Liddle burnt mound, South Ronaldsay (no. 71)

Plan of cooking shelter at Liddle (no. 71)

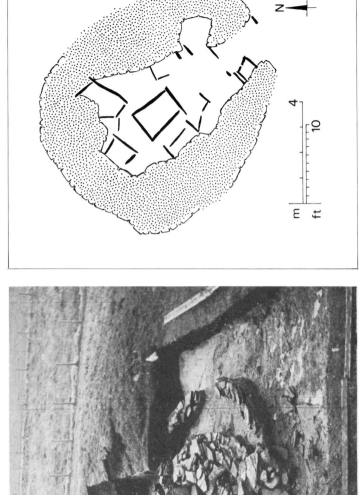

Skara Brae from the air: house 8 on the left (no. 72)

72* Skara Brae, Settlement, Orkney

c 2500 BC–c 3100 BC.
HY 231187. Well signposted from several directions, the car park for Skara Brae is on the Bay of Skaill, beside the B 9056, on the W coast of mainland. A footpath leads along the shore to the site on the S side of the bay.
HBM (SDD).

The west coast of Orkney is mostly very rugged, with high cliffs and pounding Atlantic waves prohibiting coastal settlement, and the only shelter to be found is in the three bays of Birsay, Marwick and Skaill. But the size and shape of these bays has been altered by erosion over the centuries, and the settlement of Skara Brae, when it was founded some 5000 years ago, was certainly not on the shore as it is now but set well back—indeed environmental evidence even suggests that a freshwater loch, like the Loch of Skaill behind Skaill House, may have separated the site from the sea and its immediate sandy shore. The name Skara Brae was originally coined to describe the huge sand-dune that covered the site until storm damage in 1850 revealed the presence of stone structures and midden deposits, and, although erosion has destroyed the northern margin of the settlement, it seems likely that the impression given by the visible surviving remains is essentially accurate: this was, architecturally and socially, a tightly knit housing complex for a small community of perhaps fifty people.

Radiocarbon dating suggests that Skara Brae was inhabited for around 600 years, during which time there was rebuilding and modification of the houses and interconnecting passages, and inevitably most of the structures visible today represent the final layout of the village. Its focus consists of six square or rectangular houses linked by narrow irregular passages, very much an inward-looking complex, with a single isolated building of somewhat different design on the west side of the village. The evidence of burnt stones and chips of chert found in this building (no. 8) suggests that it was not an ordinary house but a workshop, probably where chert tools were manufactured (chert was used as a substitute for flint, which in Orkney occurs only as relatively small nodules washed up on the shore). The main group of domestic houses has two remarkable characteristics: embedded in midden, it is virtually subterranean, and the internal design of its housing units has a standard uniformity. Both aspects were deliberate and, assuming that there was no prehistoric equivalent of a modern building contractor at work here, they must indicate a very strong sense of corporate identity amongst the families of this community.

house-interiors, again a contrast that must have been deliberate and which mirrors the design of contemporary tombs with their low tunnel-like passages and soaring chambers. It is as if the ideology of their builders demanded that getting there should be humiliatingly difficult but living there, whether in life or death, should be glorious. Small cells were built into the walls, mostly for storage but some furnished with drains as lavatories. A large square hearth with stone kerbs occupies the centre of each house, and the use of stone slabs to build furniture has left us with an unusually precise picture of how the rest of the room was arranged (best seen in nos 1 and 7): slab-built beds flanked either side of the hearth, and a stone dresser was built against the wall opposite the door. Wall cupboards and stone boxes sunk into the floor provide extra storage space. To these bare essentials the visitor's eye should add heather and furs to the beds, skin canopies spanning the bed-posts, decorative pottery jars to the dresser, flame to the hearth, dried meats and fish hanging from the rafters . . . .

Traces of earlier houses suggest a greater variety of plan and perhaps less sophisticated interior design: no. 9 is the most completely surviving, and it has a central hearth and bed-alcoves built into the thickness of the walls. Without demolishing the later houses, it is impossible to reconstruct the appearance of the original village, but the basic economy and material culture of the community seems to have changed little over the centuries, suggesting that the overall form of the settlement probably also remained the same. A self-sufficient life-style was based on animal husbandry, fishing and cereal cultivation, with thriving local manufacture of stone and bone tools and of thick pottery jars known as Grooved Ware, often decorated in relief with spirals, bosses and linear motifs. There is a small site museum (where an excellent official guidebook is sold) and other finds from the excavations are in Stromness Museum and Tankerness House Museum, although the bulk of the material is in RMS.

Skara Brae: main passage (no. 72)

Each house consists of a single room with thick drystone walls surviving in some places as high as 3 m. There is a marked contrast between the cramped conditions of the passageways and the equally low and narrow doorways and the spacious and comfortable

Skara Brae: house 1 (no. 72)

Skara Brae: house 1, entrance on left (no. 72)

73 Knap of Howar, Settlement, Papa Westray, Orkney

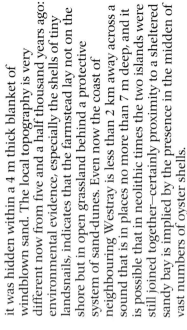

c 2800 BC–3700 BC.

HY 483518. The island can be reached by air or sea from Kirkwall: the airfield is within easy walking distance of the site, and transport to Holland from the pier at the S end can be arranged on arrival. A signposted track leads from Holland to the field in which the site lies.
HBM (SDD).

Approaching across the field, this well-preserved neolithic farmstead is invisible until the visitor is almost upon it, for it lies in a sand-filled pocket of the landscape and, until first excavated in the early 1930s,

it was hidden within a 4 m thick blanket of windblown sand. The local topography is very different now from five and a half thousand years ago: environmental evidence, especially the shells of tiny landsnails, indicates that the farmstead lay not on the shore but in open grassland behind a protective system of sand-dunes. Even now the coast of neighbouring Westray is less than 2 km away across a sound that is in places no more than 7 m deep, and it is possible that in neolithic times the two islands were still joined together—certainly proximity to a sheltered sandy bay is implied by the presence in the midden of vast numbers of oyster shells.

This was a small, single-family farmstead relying for a living on breeding cattle and sheep, fishing and growing wheat and barley. The two oblong buildings represent a dwelling-house and a multi-purpose workshop-cum-barn, built side by side with an interconnecting passage allowing access from one to another; they were not the first structures on the site, for they were built into an existing midden, but any earlier buildings were either dismantled or have yet to be discovered. This midden material, compacted into a dense clayey consistency, provided an economic building material, for the thick house-walls have a core of midden, faced on either side with stone.

The dwelling-house is the larger and best-preserved of the two buildings, with its entrance intact and its walls up to 1.6 m high; the doorway at the inner end of the lintelled entrance-passage is furnished with a sill, jambs and checks to take a wooden door which would be barred into position. Inside, the house is spacious, 10 m by 5 m, and divided by upright stone slabs (and, originally, timber posts) into two rooms, the outer having a low stone bench along one wall and the inner acting as the kitchen: excavation revealed traces of a central hearth, footings for wooden benches and post-holes for roof-supports. The great stone quern is still where it was found, along with another smaller quern: a rubbing-stone held in the hand would grind the

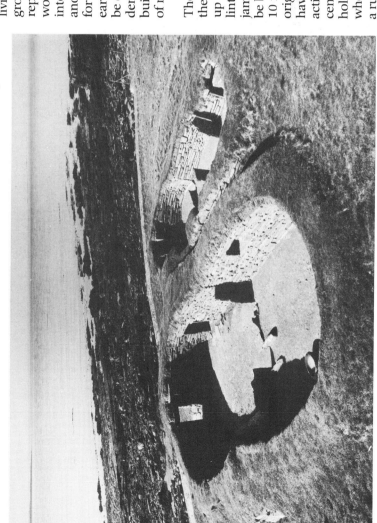

Knap of Howar neolithic farmstead, Papa Westray (no. 73)

Knap of Howar: entrance into dwelling-house (no. 73)

Neolithic settlement at Gruting School, Shetland: house in foreground (no. 74)

grain in the hollowed trough. The workshop alongside has a similar though less well-preserved main entrance and, unexpectedly, the door closing the interlinking passage between the two buildings was set in the workshop rather than in the house. Here slabs divide the interior into three rooms, the innermost furnished with shelves and cupboards and the middle room acting as the main working area, round a central stone-built hearth.

Many domestic artefacts were recovered: bone and stone tools, sherds of decorative bowls and jars (known as Unstan Ware), all made on the site from local materials (RMS).

74 Gruting School, Settlement, Shetland
3rd millennium BC.
HU 281498. On the A 971 Lerwick to Walls road, take the minor road about 1 km E of Bridge of Walls which leads SE to West Houlland and Gruting. After 1.5 km, Gruting School is on the right of the road beside Scutta Voe, and the neolithic settlement lies along the hillside between here and the head of the voe.

There are two oval houses associated with small cairns of stones cleared from the fields, but the slope is so littered with boulders from the steep hillside above that it takes some time to pick out the man-made outlines. The best-preserved house lies to the north of the road, below the second telegraph pole counting north-eastwards from the school; the basal courses of its oval wall are clearly visible, together with the entrance at the downslope end. The oval chamber has a small cell opening off its uphill end (now filled with tumbled stones) and a stone bench recessed into its eastern wall. A second house of similarly oval shape is bisected by the road just before it crosses the burn at the head of Scutta Voe, and a third lies beneath the garage near the school.

preserved examples of early houses (the huge rectangular pile of stones close to the 'Benie Hoose' represents the debris removed from the house and a superimposed planticrue by the excavators). Both houses are aligned downslope with their entrances facing east and seawards, probably to help drainage, and the builders of the 'Benie Hoose' had to cut back into the hillside to achieve a level platform. The use of massive boulders in the thick walls led to the local name 'Standing Stones of Yoxie' for the lower house, because before excavation the tips of these sometimes pointed boulders protruded well above the turf. Both structures consist of a dwelling house with one or two rooms and alcoves, and a long entrance passage leading out into an oval and probably unroofed courtyard, which is large enough to have been used as a small animal pen.

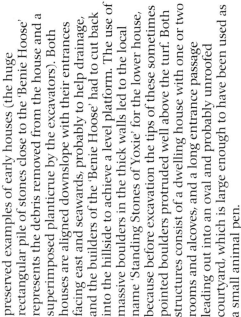

75 Pettigarths Field, Settlement, Whalsay, Shetland

3rd-2nd millennium BC.

Houses HU 586652 and 587652, tomb HU 584653.
On the slope above Yoxie Geo on the E coast of the island, about 1 km S of Muckle Breck on the Brough-Skaw road.

These two houses, known respectively as the 'Benie Hoose' and the 'Standing Stones of Yoxie', have been excavated and left open, so that they are clear and well-

Neolithic house, Pettigarths Field, Whalsay: 'Standing Stones of Yoxie' in foreground, 'Benie Hoose' in middle distance, cairns on horizon to right (no. 75)

Both houses yielded broken pottery and stone tools, but the 'Benie Hoose' was littered with an astonishing total of more than 1,800 hammerstones, pounders, stone discs and other types of large tools, including many querns, all of which indicate a long period of occupation.

This flourishing and self-sufficient small community built its own burial-place overlooking the houses and fields, and this too reflects a long history for it consists of a chambered tomb and a later cist alongside. Both are very modest in size and design, and much of their stonework must have been removed in antiquity for dyke-building, for excavation has laid bare only their basal courses amidst a spread of tumbled stones.
Originally the cairn covering the tomb was square and the entrance, facing the sea, leads through a narrow passage into a small oval chamber with three burial recesses divided off by large slabs protruding from the walls. Immediately to the north was later built a round cairn covering a large cist built with four massive slabs; the covering slab has slipped into the cist. Nothing is known about the original burials, unfortunately, because both tomb and cist had been thoroughly

143

Plan of neolithic house, 'Standing Stones of Yoxie' (no. 75)

Plan of Pettigarths Field cairns (no. 75)

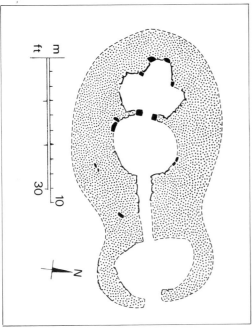

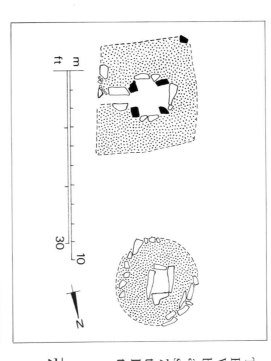

disturbed before excavation, but the two structures demonstrate as clearly as a modern graveyard the changing fashions in funerary architecture and rites over the years.

76 Pinhoulland, Settlement, Shetland

3rd-2nd millennium BC.
HU 259497. On the W side of the Voe of Browland, about 1.5 km S of Bridge of Walls on the A 971 Lerwick to Walls and Sandness road.

The quickest route is due east from the farm of Pinhoulland, but to walk along the hillside above the Voe, having first visited Scord of Brouster (no. 77), is to become immersed in the prehistoric landscape. This is a nucleated settlement of seven well-preserved houses, some of a size equalling the great Stanydale house (no. 78), the whole complex, although unexcavated, with the appearance of having been inhabited over a very long period. Large clearance cairns and low field-walls testify to considerable agricultural activity.

77 Scord of Brouster, Settlement, Shetland

3rd-2nd millennium BC.
HU 255516. On the A 971 from Lerwick to Walls and Sandness, take the Sandness fork at Bridge of Walls; the site is on the hillside above Brouster farm, to the N of the road, almost 0.5 km from the bridge.

This is perhaps the most complete and comprehensible neolithic settlement complex in Shetland. The outlines of the houses, the enclosures and the many clearance cairns are readily discernible, even from the road, and recent excavations have laid bare many details of the settlement. The most obvious enclosure is close to the road, an irregular oval almost 60 m long enclosed by a stone wall, and a large oval house is attached to its north end. The entrance is at the downslope end of the house, and the interior, 7 m by 5 m, contains a central hearth and stone-built cells lining the walls, using massive boulders as subdividing piers. A radiocarbon date places the occupation of the house in the late 3rd-early 2nd millennium BC, but the

Stones of Stenness, Orkney
(no. 84)

site as a whole is likely to span a long period. At least three other houses lie further north, and their fields cover an area of about 2 ha. Close to the first house is a perfect circular ring cairn with a kerb of large boulders.

78 Stanydale, Settlement, Shetland
3rd millennium BC.

HU 285502. The route to Stanydale is well signposted from the A 971 Lerwick to Walls road, where a minor road leading S leaves the main road some 3 km W of Bixter. The footpath over rough moorland is marked by black and white poles. HBM (SDD).

The focus of this group of monuments is an astonishing structure known as the Stanydale 'temple', a house so large and so clearly related in design to heel-shaped tombs that it must be allowed a special status: perhaps the hall of a chieftain, a tribal assembly-house, or a temple. It is accompanied by four smaller houses of the normal oval type, a system of field-walls and many clearance cairns; given the blanket peat that has developed in this relatively low-lying pocket of land, the complex may well be more extensive than is visible on the ground today. The 'temple' and one of the smaller houses have been excavated, though only the 'temple' has been partially restored, and the excavated house is the first monument encountered along the footpath.

It lies beside the third route-pole, and its plan is very clear, with walls surviving to a height of about 1 m; the entrance is downslope at the south end, entered through a porch, which would provide extra storage space as well as acting as a wind-break. Within the thick walls, which have an earthen core between stone faces, the house interior consists of a large room with a small cell at the far end, two alcoves built into the east wall, an almost central hearth and a stone bench along the west wall.

Neolithic settlement at Scord of Brouster, Shetland, during excavation (no. 77): house 1

Scord of Brouster, ring cairn (no. 77)

Interior of neolithic hall, Stanydale (no. 78)

Some very large boulders were used at the base of the house wall, but in comparison the architecture of the 'temple' is on an altogether more massive and truly megalithic scale. It presents a daunting façade, a smooth curve of drystone walling broken by a central entrance passage; the wall has been restored to a height of about 1.5 m, and the internal face includes some huge boulders estimated to weigh over 300 kg. The entrance passage is furnished with substantial inner and outer sill-stones, and it is likely that a portable wooden door would have been barred against the inner or outer end of the passage as required. Inside there is a single large hall, with two large axial post-holes for timbers supporting the ridge-beam of the roof, probably a turf-covered timber-framed roof. Fragments of wood surviving from one of these posts proved to be spruce and must have been driftwood borne across the Atlantic from North America. The hall is oval, and its inner half is furnished with six alcoves, symmetrically arranged and separated by stone piers; there is no central hearth but a series of small peripheral hearths (no longer visible). Stone tools and pottery were found, but no real hint of the purpose for which the building was designed apart from a pile of burnt sheep bones, which might perhaps point to some ritual activity (bone does not normally become charred in the cooking process).

The clearest section of field-wall is crossed by the footpath just downslope from the 'temple'; it leads away to the south-west where a series of enclosures are visible. Stanydale is separated from the Gruting School settlement (no. 74) by a high ridge known as The Hamars, on the crest of which, and visible from Stanydale, there is a large cairn surrounded by a megalithic necklace of boulders. Many stones have been robbed to build the adjacent sheep stell but the site remains impressive (HU 284500).

BURIAL MOUNDS AND ROCK CARVINGS

By the early second millennium BC, the practice of cremating human remains and burying them in small pits or stone-lined cists or boxes beneath mounds had been widely adopted in the Northern Isles. In Orkney the covering mound tends to be of earth or earth and stones (a barrow), whereas in Shetland it tends to be stone-built (a cairn), and, although many barrows have suffered erosion from ploughing, good examples of both barrows and cairns may be seen. Gravegoods are normally few in number and poor in quality (a few sherds of pottery, a steatite bowl or a stone disc would be typical finds from excavations), but there is one outstanding exception in the beautifully decorated gold discs and amber beads from Knowes of Trotty (no. 80). Burial mounds can occur singly or in groups, sometimes large groups as on the north end of the island of Papa Westray, where there are about forty mounds; such groups should be seen as cemeteries and may have remained in use over several centuries. The great ceremonial centre of Brodgar and Stenness in Orkney (nos 82,83) acted as a focus for some remarkably large and complex types of barrow,

unfortunately dug into long ago so that virtually nothing is known of their date and significance. In Shetland, the cairns tend to be located on hilltops, but this impression may be biassed if there are mounds buried beneath the peat, as seems very likely. Some of the cairns that contain stone-built cists of massive proportions may be related to neolithic chambered tombs, for multiple inhumation burials in such cists are known to have taken place in neolithic times.

The fashion for rock art that produced startling great expanses of carving in Argyll seem not to have taken a strong hold in the Northern Isles. There is just one example of cup-marks carved on a living rock-face on Whalsay (no. 82), which resemble closely the cup-marks of bronze-age date elsewhere in Scotland, and the cups and rings carved on detached boulders, as seen re-used at Midhowe (no. 60), are likely to be of somewhat later date. More ambitious in concept and technique are the decorative designs carved on earlier neolithic chambered tombs, although only on the Holm of Papa Westray (no. 92) can they be seen in position on the walls of the tomb—the magnificent stone discovered recently from a destroyed tomb at Pierowall on Westray can be admired in Tankerness House Museum, its carving beautifully crisp.

Incised slab from Ness of Brodgar, Orkney

147

79 Kirkbister Hill, Barrows, Orkney ♿³

2nd millennium BC.

HY 284263. At Twatt, on the A 986 from Kirkwall to Birsay, take a minor road NNE between the Lochs of Boardhouse and Hundland towards Swannay.

On the gentle south-eastern slopes of Kirkbister Hill is a fine group of at least ten barrows, mostly 6 m to 9 m in diameter; none of which has been excavated. This is one of several barrow cemeteries in the area; another is visible from the A 987 on the west side of the Loch of Boardhouse, on the very lowest slope of Ravie Hill. Eight mounds can be seen between the road and the loch, and it is clear from the hollows in their crests that they have suffered from the 19th century preoccupation with opening barrows, but the ninth, behind the modern house of Queenafold, was excavated in the 1960s. The earthen mound had a rough kerb of small stones at its perimeter and a central cist (now rebuilt beside the house); buried in the cist were the cremated remains of an adult male, an adult female and a deer, together with some of the charcoal from the funeral pyre, a sherd of pottery and a stone disc.

80 Knowes of Trotty, Barrows, Orkney ♿⁴

2nd millennium BC.

HY 342172–342176. On the A 986 some 4 km SE of Dounby, take a minor road leading E toward Evie; after about 2.5 km is the entry to Huntscarth and Netherhouse, and the barrows are S of the latter.

The Ward of Redland is a conspicuous hill, about 200 m high, and it is noticeable that the barrow-builders had no interest in height or maximum visability, for the mounds are ranged along the foot of the hill. There are twelve earthen mounds, the largest of which is situated closest to the farm of Netherhouse and is about 18 m in diameter and 3 m high; it covered a cist, excavated in 1858, which contained cremated bones, four gold discs and a number of amber beads and pendants (these are in the RMS). The thin gold discs are thought to have been covers for buttons, and their decoration makes an Irish origin likely for them—the gold sheeting has been hammered on a wooden mould to produce concentric circles of relief decoration—while the amber was probably imported from the Baltic. Such finds belong to a context in the early 2nd millennium BC and they suggest not only that this was the first barrow of the group to be raised but also that it commemorates someone of high and wealthy social status.

81 Nesbister Hill, Cairn, Shetland ♿⁴

2nd millennium BC.

HU 403454. On the summit of Nesbister Hill, a walk of about 0.5 km SSW from the A 971, some 13 km from Lerwick.

Of all the hilltop cairns in Shetland, Nesbister has been chosen as a good example to visit not only because it is reasonably well-preserved but also because the walk along the ridge is not arduous. Both its location and its architectural design are close to megalithic tradition, for the circular cairn, almost 8 m in diameter, has a drystone kerb and the central cist is built of massive slabs—the cist is visible now but originally it would have been covered by the stones of the cairn. Nothing is known of what was found in the cist or of when it was opened.

82 Brough, Cup-marked Rocks, Whalsay, Shetland. ♿³

2nd millennium BC.

HU 555651. On a knoll crowned with a television aerial beside the road.

The bare rock-faces on the east side of this knoll display two well-preserved groups of pecked cup-marks, about 30 in all, but they lack the elaboration of rings and other markings found elsewhere in Scotland. The lower group includes three joined in a trefoil shape.

CEREMONIAL CIRCLES AND STANDING STONES

The two henges and stone circles of the Ring of Brodgar (no. 83) and the Stones of Stenness (no. 84) should be viewed together, along with their attendant standing stones and barrows, as a great ceremonial complex in the heart of Orkney, comparable to Callanish on Lewis in the Western Isles and to Stonehenge on Salisbury Plain in Wiltshire. Henges are a purely British phenomenon, occurring as far apart as Cornwall and Orkney (none has yet been found in Shetland) and dating to the 3rd millennium BC; they consist of a circular or oval bank with a ditch outside its circumference and one or two entrance causeways. Sometimes they contain circles of standing stones, as at Brodgar and Stenness, and sometimes, in more southerly areas where timber is a more appropriate building material, excavation has revealed the post-holes of timber circles. The labour and organisation involved in the construction of these two monuments was immense: it has been estimated that cutting the Brodgar ditch involved shifting some 4,700 cubic metres of rock and would have taken about 80,000 man-hours to complete. The concept and construction of such public works imply an organised society united in its cosmology and perhaps united in its allegiance to a high king; it has been argued that, in Orkney, society evolved from small autonomous groups in early neolithic times to a centralized, hierarchical tribal system in the early 3rd millennium. The sanctity of the Brodgar-Stenness area remained potent throughout the 3rd and 2nd millennia, as the various burial mounds and standing stones testify; a cemetery of small stone cists discovered in 1925 yielded an elegantly decorated slab, incised with chevrons and lozenges.

Standing stones, sometimes in pairs but normally single, occur frequently both in Orkney and Shetland, but none has been scientifically investigated and little is known of their purpose or precise date. They are usually set up in conspicuous positions, although not necessarily on the crest of hills or ridges, and the tallest can be 3 m to 5.6 m high above the surface of the ground, implying that their total length, including the portion underground, may well be over 6 m in many cases. Sometimes the tops of the chocking stones are visible, jammed into the pit into which the monolith was set to keep it upright. From evidence elsewhere in Scotland, such stones may be associated with burials and there is some support for this idea in the Northern Isles: pairs of stones at Brodgar (no. 83) and Beorgs of Housetter (no. 87) appear to be associated with burial mounds. It is also possible that they were set up as markers of one sort or another, territorial or astronomical, and, on balance, a date in the second millennium BC is most likely, but standing stones are particularly tantalising fragments of an ancient landscape that we cannot hope ever to understand entirely. Several stones have become part of local folklore—Giant's Stones being a frequent name for them—and have even been used in old customs until within the last century, particularly in the plighting of troths between lovers.

---

83 **Ring of Brodgar, Henge and Stone Circle, Orkney**
3rd millennium BC.
HY 294133. On the A 965, Stromness to Kirkwall road, take the B 9055 NW between the lochs of Stenness and Harray; the Ring is clearly visible on the left and is signposted.
HBM (SDD).

The Ness of Brodgar was a perfect place to choose for a great ceremonial monument, giving the impression of being surrounded by water and sky and yet firmly in the fertile heart of Orkney. Its open location is

Map of the Brodgar-Stenness ceremonial complex, Orkney

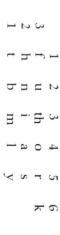

Ring of Brodgar runes (no. 83)

echoed by the vastness of the circle. In essence, this is a henge monument with two entrances enclosing a perfect circle of standing stones, 103.7 m in diameter; there is no trace of a bank, despite the great volume of rock and soil that must have been dug out of the ditch, about 10 m wide at ground-level and more than 3 m deep (now half-full of silt). In the mid 19th century only fourteen stones were standing, but others have been re-erected so that there are twenty-seven standing, and the positions are known of another thirteen; assuming that the stones were put up at approximately equal distances, it is likely that there were originally sixty stones in the circle. Apart from those surviving as broken stumps, the existing stones vary between about 2 m and 4.5 m in height. It has been suggested that the circle was designed as a lunar observatory, using the Hellia Cliff on Hoy which is outlined on the horizon as a foresight, but the date at which this could have been possible is calculated at c 1500 BC, which is almost certainly much later than the date of construction – as yet there is no precise

dating evidence but the early to mid 3rd millennium would be the most likely context. There has been no excavation within the circle to discover whether any trace exists of internal structures. Sometime in the 12th century, a Norse visitor carved his name on the south face of one of the stones in the northernmost arc of the circle (the third stone to the north of the entrance); the stone is now a broken stump, but his runic letters are clear, together with a small cross incised beneath them. These are twig runes or tree runes, so called from their appearance, and they are cryptographic but easily read by counting the branches on either side of each rune and then reading off the numbers on the following table: counting (from the right) gives 12 (mistakenly written 21 on the rune) 23 34 r (as an ordinary rune) 22. Reading from the left-hand side and then the top of the table, these pairs of numbers give biorn, a common man's name even today, Bjorn.

	1	2	3	4	5	6
3	f	u	th	o	r	k
2	h	n	i	a	s	
1	t	b	m	l	y	

There are two very large burial mounds to the north-east of the Ring of Brodgar, between the modern road and the loch, and another large mound, known as Salt Knowe, to the west; smaller mounds are scattered over the Ness of Brodgar from south of the great circle to the Ring of Bookan to the north, but very little is known of their contents or date. The Ring of Bookan may be another, smaller henge monument (HY 283144), while to the immediate east of the Ring of Brodgar is a standing stone known as the Comet Stone, set on a low platform on which the stumps of two more stones are visible. A pair of standing stones, some 8 m apart, adorn the very tip of the promontory near Brodgar farm (HY 303128). It seems likely that in prehistoric times the promontories of Brodgar and Stenness were still joined as a narrow neck of land.

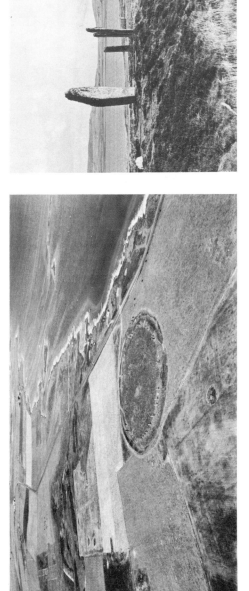

Aerial view of the Ring of Brodgar (no. 83) and adjacent burial mounds

Ring of Brodgar (no. 83), Comet Stone in middle distance and Maes Howe in background to right

Ring of Brodgar (no. 83)

84 The Stones of Stenness, Henge and Stone Circle, Orkney

Early 3rd millennium BC.
HY 306125. On the A 965, Stromness to Kirkwall road, take the B 9055 NW for just over 0.5 km; the site is close to the E side of the road; signposted. HBM (SDD).

After suffering deliberate destruction of two of its stones and one of its outlying standing stones (the Stone of Odin) in the early 19th century, restoration was carried out in the early 20th century and four stones of the circle now survive, the tallest over 5 m high. Excavation revealed the bedding-holes for other stones, and it is likely that there were originally twelve stones set in a circle about 30 m in diameter. Although ploughing has all but levelled the henge earthworks, the circle once stood within a ditch and bank with an overall diameter of about 44 m and an entrance causeway on the north, and excavation has shown the ditch to be 7 m wide at ground-level and over 2 m deep, cut into solid rock. In the centre of the circle was found a square setting of flat slabs and, aligned between this and the entrance, the bedding slots for a series of stone and timber uprights, but none of these last features is now visible.

Bones of cattle, sheep and dog were found in the bottom of the ditch—along with one human finger-bone—and radiocarbon analysis of the bones indicates that the henge was built in the early 3rd millennium BC, a date confirmed by discovery of Grooved Ware pottery similar to that from the contemporary village of Skara Brae, some 10 km to the north-west.

Two outlying standing stones are likely to have some connection with the henge: the Watch Stone, a magnificent slab, 5.6 m tall, which stands close to the causeway between the two promontories, and the Barnhouse Stone, some 700 m south-east of the circle.

85 Stane O'Quoybune, Orkney

2nd millennium BC.

HY 253263. On the A 967 between Twatt and Birsay, at the NW extreme of the Loch of Boardhouse, in a field immediately SW of the main road.

This is a very fine standing stone, almost 4 m high, which may well be contemporary with some of the burial mounds around the Loch of Boardhouse, particularly those below Ravie Hill (see no. 79). Local folklore relates that this stone goes down to the loch for a drink early on New Year's morning, though it must be back in its place by dawn; this is a common folktale told of several stones, sometimes with the additional caution that anyone happening to see the stone in action will not live to celebrate the following New Year.

86 Stone of Setter, Eday, Orkney

2nd millennium BC.

Hy 564371. On the B 9063 some 1.5 km S of Calf Sound, take the minor road NW past Mill Loch; the stone is to the immediate N of the road at the N end of the loch.

Weathering has so furrowed this monolith as to give it a most formidably ancient appearance, enhancing its height (4.5 m) and dominating position overlooking several chambered tombs and Calf Sound to the north (see Eday excursion). Its careful location makes clear the intention of those who set it up that it should become a focal point in the island landscape as viewed from the north and perhaps even from the sea, whence it has certainly taken on the status of a familiar landmark.

153

Stones of Stenness (no. 84)

The Stone of Setter, Eday (no. 86)

87 Beorgs of Housetter, Standing Stones, Shetland

2nd millennium BC.

HU 361854. Beside the A 970 from Lerwick, some 7 km before it terminates at Isbister.

Known locally as the Giant's Grave, this monument has an extraordinary setting: it stands on a narrow strip of boulder-strewn land between the Loch of Housetter on the east and the Beorgs of Housetter on the west, a most precipitous rocky hillside that acts as a backdrop to this natural theatre—not even the modern road that now crosses the stage can detract from its dramatic effect. And the builders of the Giant's Grave enhanced that effect by using the two colours of granitic rock that outcrop on the Beorgs hillside: the two standing stones are red, while the cairn between them is built predominantly of white rock that weathers to pale grey. The standing stones are broad slabs aligned north-south, 2 m and 2.7 m high respectively, and they appear as sentinels to the ruinous cairn at their feet; a massive low slab set upright within the mass of stones in the cairn may represent one side of a former cist, and there is a hint of a formal kerb round the perimeter of the cairn.

About 90 m to the north of the Giant's Grave are the remains of a chambered tomb, familiarly known as the Towie Knowe or Fairy Mound—both tomb and the cairn to the south have been used as convenient sources of road metal in the past, and the tomb has also been dug into by early antiquaries. It is now an amorphous spread of stones, but it appears to have been a heel-shaped cairn with a central chamber opening to the east.

88 Busta, Standing Stone, Shetland

2nd millennium BC.

HU 348673, on the A 970 between Voe and Hillswick take the minor road about 1 km beyond Brae which leads S along the W side of Busta Voe; the stone is in a field on the E side of the road a short distance from the junction.

This is a very impressive standing stone in a spectacular situation overlooking Busta Voe. A stout monolith of granite which is thought to weigh some 20 tons, this stone must have required considerable labour and effort to erect, and it is interesting to see the top layer of stones used to wedge it into position in its pit. Immediately to the north-east there is another smaller stone, a squat triangular block, which must also have been brought deliberately to this spot. Popular tradition has it that the larger stone was thrown here in anger by the Devil from some hill in Northmavine.

89 Uyea Breck, Standing Stone, Unst, Shetland

2nd millennium BC.

HP 604005. From the A 968, take the B 9084 to the pier at Uyeasound, and follow the minor road round the bay towards Muness; the site lies S of the road, about 1.5 km beyond the pier.

Most of the island's standing stones are squat boulders, though they can be as massive as one of the Bordastubble stones at 3.6 m high and a girth of 6.7 m (HP 578033), but this is a slender monolith, 3 m high, set on a slope overlooking Skuda Sound and the island of Uyea.

CHAMBERED CAIRNS

The architectural resemblances between domestic houses and chambered tombs make clear that, in the minds of their builders, tombs were houses of the dead: compare Knap of Howar (no. 73) with Knowe of Yarso (no. 94) and Skara Brae (no. 72) with Maes Howe (no. 95). Their basic designs are related, the shape of the tombs mirroring that of the houses, and floor space is created and used in the same way—upright slabs divide the Knap of Howar houses into rooms and the chambers of stalled cairns into compartments. Both were long-term, permanent structures used by many generations. Chambered tombs were a combination of the family burial vault and the ossuary, designed to be used over and over again, their entrances sealed between burials. Over the centuries their contents changed, and, even where a tomb has been found intact and scientifically excavated (unfortunately many were disturbed long ago), there can be no telling how much rearrangement or even spring-cleaning has taken place during its lifetime. The number of burials can vary from single figures to three figures, but they seem to be proportionate to the size of tomb, and the fact that men, women and children are represented implies that this was not a special form of burial confined to chieftains. In most cases the skeletons are both disarticulated and very incomplete; at Quanterness (see no. 100) and Isbister (no. 93) the evidence has been attributed to the practice of excarnation

(exposing the corpses to natural processes of defleshing before burial in the tomb), but elsewhere, particularly at Midhowe (no. 96), the latest burials were complete articulated skeletons whereas earlier ones had been sorted and rearranged.

The majority of Orcadian chambered tombs belong to a design known as the Orkney-Cromarty type, prevalent both in Orkney and on the northern mainland of Scotland, in which a passage leads into a chamber divided into compartments by upright slabs; most of the examples described here are stalled cairns, in which the chamber is elongated into as many as the fourteen compartments of Midhowe (no. 96). The heel-shaped cairns of Shetland, such as Punds Water (no. 103), are related to this basic Orkney-Cromarty design, though the difference in the available building stone can make the Shetland tombs look relatively primitive. Some twelve tombs in Orkney belong to the Maes Howe type, in which a passage opens into a large square or rectangular chamber, the walls of which have small entrances into side-cells. The tombs described in detail below are heavily weighted towards Orkney, not because there are markedly more tombs there than in Shetland but because they are better preserved and more extensively restored—Shetland stone has inhibited both ancient builders and modern conservationists. It is advisible to take a large torch and water-proof trousers when visiting chambered cairns, for most are dark and many involve crawling on invariably wet floors.

90* Cuween Hill, Chambered Cairn, Orkney

3rd millennium BC.
HY 364127. On the A 965 Kirkwall to Finstown road, take the signposted minor road just south of Finstown and, after 1 km, a track leading to the house where the key is kept.

You must enter this tomb as did neolithic man, uncomfortably on your hands and knees! But it is worth the effort, not just to see the burial chamber but also to appreciate the psychology behind the design of the tomb and the practical difficulties of any funerary rituals. This is a Maes Howe type of chamber, set within a circular cairn; the main chamber has four side-cells, one of them double, and the quality of the masonry is very high. When first explored in the 19th century, the skulls of twenty-four dogs were found on the floor of the chamber, perhaps as a token of tribal identity.

91 Dwarfie Stane, Rock-cut Tomb, Hoy, Orkney

3rd millennium BC.
HY 243004. The ferry from Stromness lands at Mo Ness on the NE coast of the island; take the B 9049 S for 2 km and then the minor road S towards Rackwick for another 2 km. The site is visible on the hillside to the S of the road; signposted.
HBM (SDD).

As the only chambered tomb known on Hoy, it is perhaps fitting that the Dwarfie Stane should be an oddity. Its builders, or rather carvers, used an isolated natural block of sandstone to hollow out of the solid rock a small chamber, with two side-cells entered over the projecting sills. A large boulder lying outside the entrance is the original blocking stone, which is recorded as having been seen in position in the 16th century, but nothing is known of the contents of the tomb. Hollowing out this tomb must have been an extraordinary task for just a few people at a time—the marks of their stone tools can be seen on the roof of the south cell.

92 Holm of Papa Westray South, Chambered Cairn, Papa Westray, Orkney

3rd millennium BC.

HY 509518. At the S end of the Holm of Papay, a small island off the E coast of Papa Westray; enquire at the Papay Community Co-operative for a boat.

HBM (SDD).

It is likely that, in neolithic times, Holm of Papay was not an island but a promontory attached at the north end to Papa Westray, but even so it must be regarded as an uncommonly remote place to find one of the largest and most extraordinary tombs in Orkney. It is essentially a Maes Howe design, with side-cells opening off a main rectangular chamber, but the enclosing cairn is oblong rather than round simply as the most economic way to encompass an enormously elongated chamber, fully 20.5 m in length. The

entrance-passage opens into the south-east long side of the chamber and, perhaps as a measure to strengthen the roof, there is a sub-dividing wall at either end of the chamber, each with a low doorway to allow access. No fewer than twelve side-cells, two of them double, are ranged round the chamber, all of them intact with lintelled entrances only 40 cm to 60 cm high. The roof over the main chamber is modern, and the visitor enters through a hatch and down a ladder rather than through the original low passage, although it is still complete. There are decorative carvings to discover, one on the south-east wall of the central part of the chamber, just south of the entrance, consisting of a double ring and an inverted V-motif; and three at the south-west end of the chamber, beyond the dividing wall; on the lintel over the entrance to the south-east cell there are pecked dots and arcs, some combined to make 'eye-brow' motifs which are also to be found in Irish chambered tombs, and on the opposite wall are

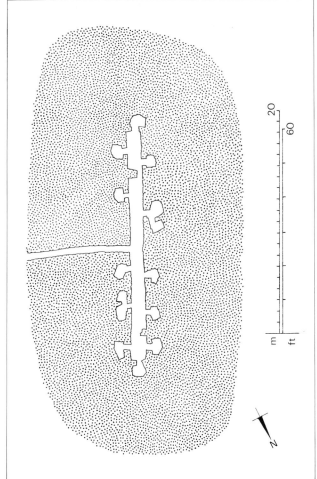

Plan of Holm of Papa Westray South chambered tomb, Orkney (no. 92)

Holm of Papa Westray South: carved design on lintel over cell-opening (no. 92)

Holm of Papa Westray North: end-cell during excavation

Holm of Papa Westray North: tomb during excavation

zig-zag and circle motifs. Nothing is known of the original contents of the tomb.

At the north end of the island is a stalled cairn known as Holm of Papa Westray North (HY 504522); it has recently been excavated and, although largely filled in again as a protective measure, the main features of the tombs are still visible (the outer wall-face was built up so that the original walling is safely beneath ground-level). The cairn is rectangular with a passage at the north end leading into a rectangular chamber, subdivided by upright slabs into four compartments which has the addition of an unusual end-cell. Traces of ancient field-walls can be seen to the south and east of the cairn.

93 Isbister, Chambered Cairn, South Ronaldsay, Orkney

3rd–late 4th millennium BC.
ND 470845. Take the A 961 from Kirkwall to its terminus at the S end of South Ronaldsay; turn E on the B 9041 for 1.5 km and then the signposted minor road S to Liddle Farm.

Like the burnt mound at Liddle (no. 71), the Isbister tomb is owned, and indeed was excavated, by the

farmer, Mr R Simison, and there is a small display of finds at the farm, where visitors will be directed or taken to the tomb. The cairn is oval, though its shape is somewhat obscured by later additions, and the entrance to the chamber faces out to sea; the tomb is now quite close to precipitous cliffs and, even allowing for erosion, its situation must always have been spectacular.

The chamber has been left open, for its roof had been removed in antiquity when the tomb was filled with stones and earth after the final burials, but two side-cells on the best-preserved western side of the chamber are intact. The design of the tomb shows it to be a hybrid, a stalled cairn furnished with side-cells in the manner of the Maes Howe type; the main chamber is divided into three compartments by pairs of upright slabs, and there are three side-cells and a shelved compartment at either end of the chamber, making an overall length of just over 8 m. Apart from the northern end-cell and the north-east side-cell, which had been disturbed and robbed prior to the excavation, the rest of the tomb and its contents were intact, and the floor deposits yielded many human and animal bones and fishbones. The two western side-cells had been used primarily for human skulls. Particularly intriguing was the inclusion of carcases and talons of sea-eagles, perhaps a totemistic feature comparable to the dog skulls at Cuween (no. 90), and Isbister has become popularly known as the Tomb of the Eagles. Analysis of the human bones suggests that around 340 people were buried in the tomb, though many individuals were represented by very few bones—it is suggested that the bodies were excarnated elsewhere, and token deposits of bones taken into the tomb. A large amount of sherds from Unstan Ware bowls was also found in the tomb, mostly in a pile in the main chamber opposite the entrance. A series of radiocarbon dates indicates a very long period of use for the tomb of around 800 years after its construction in about 3000 BC.

Isbister, South Ronaldsay: tomb during excavation (no. 93)

Isbister, South Ronaldsay: burial deposits in main chamber and side-cell (no. 93)

159

Maes Howe from the air (no. 95)

94 Knowe of Yarso, Chambered Cairn, Rousay, Orkney

3rd millennium BC.

HY 404279. Take the B 9064 from Trumland W for 2.5 km, where a signposted path leads uphill from the road to the tomb.

HBM (SDD).

The builders of this tomb chose a terrace on a steep hillside with a superb view over Eynhallow Sound, regardless of the effort involved in carrying up the slabs used in its construction. It has a stalled chamber set within a sub-rectangular cairn, and a decorative effect was achieved in the outer wall-face by setting the slabs at an angle. The chamber is protected by a modern roof, and its walls are well-preserved to a height of about 1.8 m; it is divided into three compartments, the end one double-sized but nonetheless marked off into two areas by low upright slabs. Parts of twenty-nine individuals were found in the chamber, mostly in the innermost compartment, the skulls carefully arranged against the wall, and amongst the animal bones were remains of some thirty-six deer. There was also an unusually large number of flint tools, especially scrapers, which may perhaps be connected symbolically with the deer in the sense of being tools suitable for the preparation of animal skins for clothing and other articles.

Another well-preserved stalled cairn is Blackhammer, set on a lower terrace to the south-east (HY 414276), HBM (SDD), while to the west, again on a lower terrace, are the grass-grown remains of a very long stalled cairn, Knowe of Ramsay (HY 400279), which on excavation proved to contain a chamber divided into fourteen compartments.

95* Maes Howe, Chambered Cairn, Orkney

Early 3rd millennium BC.

HY 318127. About 14.5 km WNW of Kirkwall on the A 965; signposted.

HBM (SDD).

More than any other prehistoric monument, the design and execution of Maes Howe epitomises the skill of neolithic masons in Orkney, and the tomb is rightly considered to be one of the supreme achievements of prehistoric Europe. It is inevitable that such a huge mound should have been robbed long ago, and when it was opened in 1861 by James Farrer it was indeed empty of its original contents, part of the entrance-passage has been restored, but from the door-checks inwards it is original—the great boulder in its triangular niche just inside the doorway on the left would have been drawn forwards with ropes to close the entrance. In keeping with the proportions of the tomb, the passage is quite spacious, although at a height of 1.4 m it is not possible to walk upright. Note the enormous slabs with which the passage has been constructed.

The main chamber is about 4.5 m square and was originally about the same in height, with three side-cells entered above ground-level; in each corner there is a buttress designed to help in supporting the weight of the corbelled roof. The masonry is superb, the slabs finely adjusted by underpinning or dressing to create a smooth face even where they are in fact oversailing one another towards the roof, and the tapering orthostats facing one side of each buttress not only create an impression of soaring vertical space but attractively interrupt the horizontal lines of the walls.

When Farrer dug into Maes Howe, he found that the chamber had already been broken into, as he did, from the top: from *Orkneyinga Saga* and from the runic inscriptions on the walls of the chamber, it is clear that it was entered on more than one occasion by Norsemen in the 12th century, to whom the mound was known as *Orkhaugr*. During the struggle between the rival earls Erlend and Harald for control of the earldom, Harald and some of his men sought shelter in Maes Howe from a snowstorm, but it was such a terrible experience that two of them went mad, 'which slowed them down badly' says the saga, though they still reached their destination by nightfall. The following winter of 1153-4, crusaders gathered together ready for a trip to the Holy Land broke into the chamber and incised some of the runic inscriptions, and there were probably other occasions as well when runes were cut there. This is one of the largest extant collections of runic inscriptions in the world—about thirty inscriptions at the last informed

Maes Howe: entrance into south-east cell and decorated buttress (no. 95)

Maes Howe dragon (no. 95)

apart from a fragment of human skull. Its location, close to the great ceremonial complex of the Brodgar-Stenness circles, is presumably no accident.

The mound was built on a levelled circular platform, encircled by a low bank composed of earth scraped up from a shallow ditch on its inner side; the mound itself, 35 m in diameter and 7 m high, consists largely of clay and stones, but there is an inner core of stones casing and supporting the chamber. The outermost

count, including both ordinary runes and cryptographic twig runes, and there are also some beautifully executed carvings of a walrus, a serpent knot and a dragon or lion on the north-east buttress, all in typically vigorous Scandinavian style.

Two of the most interesting inscriptions are nos 18 and 16 (the original numbering applied by Farrer is still used) on the large block on the north side of the entrance to the south-east cell and continuing on the cell lintel, which read, in a mixture of twig runes and ordinary runes: 'These runes were carved by the man most skilled in runes in the western ocean', 'with the axe which belonged to Gaukr Trandilsson in the south of Iceland'. A superb piece of genealogical detective work by a modern Icelander, Hermann Pálsson, has identified the rune-carver as Thórhallr Ásgrimsson, the great-great-great grandson of the man who slew Gaukr Trandilsson some 200 years earlier, the story of which is told in *Njals Saga*. For the archaeologist trying to use

objects as dating evidence, the thought of an axe still in use over six generations is very sobering!

Several other inscriptions mention treasure; eg 'It is long ago that a great treasure was hidden here'; 'Happy is he who might find the great treasure'. Until recently, it was assumed that this was wishful thinking and no more, as treasure to Norsemen would mean gold or silver, neither of which could have been buried with the original pre-metal neolithic occupants of the tomb. A new slant to the question arose after the recent excavations, when structural evidence for a rebuilding of the bank encircling the mound was radiocarbon dated to the 9th century AD: it now seems possible that the tomb was re-used and its external appearance improved for the burial of a Viking chieftain, whose rich grave-goods were stolen three centuries later— 'Hakon alone bore the treasure out of this mound' records one of the inscriptions, while another insists 'It is certain and true as I say, that the treasure has been moved from here. The treasure was taken away three nights before they broke into his mound'.

96 Midhowe, Chambered Cairn, Rousay, Orkney

3rd millennium BC.

HY 372304. Take the B 9064 from Trumland to a point about 2 km beyond Westness where the footpath to Midhowe broch and cairn is signposted.

HBM (SDD).

Built on low-lying ground near the sea, this excavated stalled cairn is entirely housed within a modern hangar-like building, so that it can be viewed both at ground-level and from an overhead walkway; it is a very fine monument, with an elongated chamber, 23 m in length, divided by pairs of upright slabs into twelve compartments and encased within an oblong cairn. A decorative effect has been achieved on the outer face of the cairn by setting stones at an angle, best seen almost as a herring-bone pattern on the east face. At its north-east and south-east corners, the cairn is attached to contemporary field-walls which have been traced for about 20 m and 13 m respectively, underlining the association of the tomb with its surrounding agrarian landscape.

The chamber had been filled with stones when the tomb was closed (masonry closing the passage is still in position) and the contents were undisturbed: remains of twenty-five people were found, mostly lying on or tucked beneath the shelves along the east side of the chamber, including nine complete skeletons.

Midhowe chambered cairn, Rousay (no. 96)

163

97* Quoyness, Chambered Cairn, Sanday, Orkney

3rd millennium BC.

HY 676377. Sanday can be reached by sea or air from Kirkwall; the tomb is on the Els Ness peninsula, some 6 km from Kettletoft via the B 9069 and a signposted footpath.

HBM (SDD).

The location of Quoyness is very similar to that of Holm of Papa Westray South (no. 92), on an isolated peninsula, except that Els Ness, unlike the Holm of Papay, is still, just, connected to the adjacent mainland. Both are outstanding examples of Maes Howe type tombs. Although lacking its original roof, the chamber stands intact to its full height of 4 m, and consequently the external appearance of the cairn is also very impressive, the more so as it stands on an artificial platform. Three consecutive wall-faces can be seen, representing the inner cairn round the chamber, a middle revetment flush with the outer end of the the entrance-passage and an outer casing. Originally the entrance-passage was roofed for its full length of 9 m, but only the inner 3.5 m is now intact and roofed at a height of 0.6 m—the complete 9 m crawl must have been a daunting experience!

Emerging on hands and knees, the chamber seems vast and soaring skywards. Low entrances open into six side-cells, all but two of which contained burials, and there were further burials in a cist sunk into a pit in the southern corner of the chamber–unfortunately this was a depressingly bad 19th century excavation in which an enormous amount of archaeological information was lost. Objects found in and around the tomb included bone and stone implements similar to examples from the contemporary settlement at Skara Brae (no. 72), and it is likely that the tomb was built very early in the 3rd millennium BC.

The wrecked but still impressive mound nearby to the south may well have been another chambered tomb, traditionally known as Egmondshowe (HY 676375); it

is enclosed by an arc of eleven small bronze-age burial mounds connected by a bank. At least another twenty-six small cairns are scattered over the peninsula, implying its continuing sanctity as a burial place throughout the 2nd millennium BC.

Quoyness chambered tomb,
Sanday: entrance (no. 97)

98 Taversoe Tuick, Chambered Cairn, Rousay, Orkney
3rd millennium BC.
HY 425276. Just N of the B 9064, some 1 km from the pier; signposted.
HBM (SDD).

This is one of two Orcadian tombs remarkable for their double-storey design; the other is Huntersquoy on Eday (HY 562377) of which little can now be seen. In both cases, there is an upper and a lower chamber, each with its own entrance-passage opening in diametrically opposed directions and with no access between the two, so that they are in effect two separate tombs although they appear to have been built simultaneously. At Taversoe Tuick it is possible to enter both chambers, and to look into an unusual miniature 'tomb' built at the edge of the platform on which the main tomb stands, close to the passage leading into the lower chamber. It contained three pottery bowls and may have been connected with ritual activities.

99 Vinquoy, Chambered Cairn, Eday, Orkney ⬛
3rd millennium BC.
HY 560381. On Vinquoy Hill at the N end of the island; from the B 9063, take minor road NW past Mill Loch for about 1.5 km and walk NNE along the ridge for about 0.5 km.

Set on a hilltop, this tomb commands a very extensive view over Orkney. It is a well-preserved Maes Howe type of tomb, with a main chamber and four side-cells, and it has recently been restored and opened to public view. As it was built on a slope, the tomb is partly subterranean, with its entrance downslope and a level floor created by digging back into the hillside. The main chamber must originally have been at least 3 m high, and the corbelling of its roof cannot have been an easy task given the irregular fracturing of the local stone.

100 Wideford Hill, Chambered Cairn, Orkney ⬛
3rd millennium BC.
HY 409121. Take the A 965 from Kirkwall towards Finstown for almost 8 km, then a signposted minor road SE for 2.5 km (this is the simplest rather than the quickest route); a signposted footpath leads N over rough moorland for 1.5 km.
HBM (SDD).

Though not an easy walk, the reward is a tomb in excellent condition and, on a clear day, a beautiful view over the Bay of Firth. This is another Maes Howe design and, as at Quoyness (no. 97), all three wall-faces are visible, representing the various stages of construction of the cairn. The chamber with its three side-cells is dug back into the hillside and the entrance is downslope (although entry is now through a hatch in the roof, the passage being only 0.6 m high). Excavation in the 19th century found the cells to be empty, although the main chamber had been deliberately filled with rubble.

165

Wideford Hill chambered cairn,
Orkney: entrance and walling in
cairn (no. 100)

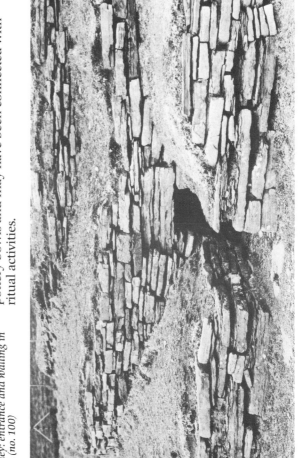

On the northern lower slope of Wideford at Quanterness (HY 417129), there is a large mound which, though inaccessible, contains a magnificent tomb of Maes Howe design, with six cells opening off the main chamber. Recent excavation of 80% of the tomb (the rest left deliberately for posterity) yielded human bones estimated to belong to 157 individuals, who had been brought into the tomb in skeletal state as at Isbister (no. 93). Unlike Wideford the tomb had not been closed by infilling. Radiocarbon dates indicate that Quanterness was built around 3400 BC and remained in use for about a thousand years.

101* Unstan, Chambered Cairn, Orkney

3rd millennium BC.

HY 282117. Just N of the A 965 some 4 km NE of Stromness; signposted.

HBM (SDD).

This is the stalled cairn after which Unstan Ware was named, for its excavation in the late 19th century yielded sherds of at least thirty-five bowls of this distinctively shaped and decorated ware. It was built on a low-lying promontory on the south shore of Loch of Stenness, mirroring the location of the Stones of Stenness (no. 84) with which the use of the tomb was almost certainly contemporary.

The circular cairn covers a chamber very similar to that at Isbister (no. 93): it is divided by upright slabs into three central compartments and two shelved end-cells, and a side-cell opens off the west wall of the central compartment. The lintel over the cell bears a brief runic inscription, but the stone is not in its original position (having been placed here during restoration); the fact that the runes are carved across the narrow face of the slab implies that it was set upright. The bird and other doodles on the same slab have apparently been added since restoration this century.

Beyond the tomb, two lines of rampart and ditch cut off the tip of the promontory; nothing is known of the date of this fortified enclosure, an unusual monument for the Northern Isles, and it is not inconceivable that it might be neolithic.

102 Gallow Hill, Chambered Cairn, Shetland

3rd-2nd millennium BC.

HU 258508. Beside the A 971 Lerwick to Walls road, less than 0.5 km beyond Bridge of Walls, the cairn is to the immediate NW of the road.

Although its situation can be appreciated from the road, the cairn itself is now so low as to be difficult to pick out against a rock-strewn slope, for the stones of the cairn may well have been robbed in antiquity to build field-walls (see no. 77). Close to, however, it is still impressive, a huge round cairn with a kerb of massive boulders about 25 m in diameter, in the centre of which there are traces of very large stones enclosing a circular chamber, but nothing is known of its contents. Standing on the cairn, it is not difficult to ignore the modern road and to appreciate the sweep of the Voe of Browland and the landscapes on either side with their marvellously preserved early prehistoric settlements and field systems (nos 74, 76). Another chambered tomb at the head of the voe on the Ward of Browland at 100 m OD (HU 267515) commands an even more extensive view over this beautiful land and seascape.

103 Punds Water, Chambered Cairn, Shetland

3rd-2nd millennium BC.

HU 324712. From the A 970 between Brae and Hillswick, a minor road some 5 km beyond Brae leads to Mangaster; about halfway along the minor road, walk WNW towards Punds Water, and the cairn is close to the S shore of the loch.

This is one of the best-preserved heel-shaped cairns, probably because it lies in what has become, since the round a central area, very reminiscent of domestic houses of the same period (HU 322714). Another heel-shaped cairn, very similar to the first Punds Water tomb, has been excavated and is still visible on the south side of the Islesburgh peninsula (about 3 km down the A 970 southwards from the Mangaster turning to Islesburgh farm, and a walk of almost 1 km south-south-west; HU 334684); this cairn is part of a well-preserved neolithic landscape that includes a house and field-walls.

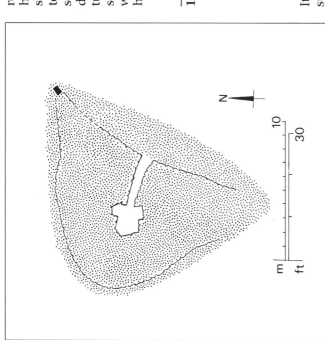

Plan of Punds Water chambered cairn, Shetland (no. 103)

104 Vementry, Chambered Cairn, Shetland

3rd-2nd millennium BC.

HU 295609. On the A 971, Lerwick to Walls road, take the B 9071 at Bixter to Aith, where a minor road leads N along Aith Voe and terminates at Vementry. The farmer, Mr I Hunter, operates a small ferry to the island.

Its remote situation has ensured that this tomb survives in excellent condition; it was built on the top of Muckle Ward, 90 m OD, and the stiff climb to reach it is rewarded in clear weather by a superb view over a beautiful area of Shetland. This is a heel-shaped cairn with a smoothly curving facade of excellent drystone walling, including very large stones at the base, which survives to a height of 1.2 m. There is no entrance through the facade, and this outer part of the cairn appears to have been built as a platform round a circular, originally domed cairn enclosing the burial chamber. A passage aligned on the centre of the facade leads into a roughly trefoil-shaped chamber, now unroofed and ruinous, although its walling is visible.

The island is also remarkable for the Second World War gun emplacements on Swarbacks Head (HU 290619). At Vementry farm on the mainland there is a well-preserved click mill (HU 311597).

formation of blanket peat, an inhospitable area of small lochs and moorland, although around 3000 years ago its potential for farming would have been considerably better. The cairn was built on a low knoll and the kerb can be traced very easily, one or more courses high, showing that the lower part of the cairn had a vertical external face (there are tumbled stones beyond the original face); in the centre of the concave facade on the ESE side is a passage leading to a trefoil-shaped burial chamber. Both chamber and passage are now roofless, but their walls will still stand over a metre in height, in places using very large stones.

A second tomb was excavated in 1959 on the west side of Punds Water, which was almost circular externally with an interior divided into five small benched cells

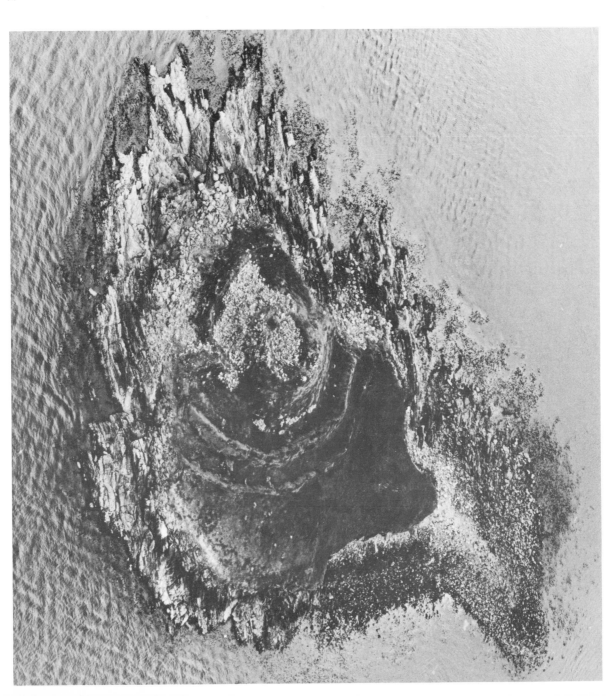

MUSEUMS

Several monuments have small displays of artefacts in site museums, including the Brough of Birsay (no. 57), the broch of Gurness (no. 59), Skara Brae (no. 72) and Isbister (no. 93) in Orkney, and Jarlshof (no. 55) in Shetland. Each of the crofts restored as museums of rural life have been treated here as monuments: Corrigall Farm Museum and Kirkbister in Orkney (nos. 27, 29; open April-September) and the Shetland Croft Museum (no. 26; open May-September). In addition to these, the Tingwall Agricultural Museum at Veensgarth, Gott, Shetland (HU 427443; privately owned, open May-September) displays 18th century agricultural implements in the outbuildings of a working croft.

Stromness Museum, Alfred Street, Stromness, Orkney, is primarily a natural history and maritime museum, including the naval history of Scapa Flow.

Tankerness House Museum, Broad Street, Kirkwall, Orkney, a fine 16th century house (no. 23), contains major archaeological collections, including finds from Skara Brae, Gurness and Buckquoy, the neolithic carved stone from Pierowall and the Pictish symbol stone from Knowe of Burrian.

Scalloway Museum, Scalloway, Shetland, displays of local history.

Shetland Museum, Lower Hillhead, Lerwick, houses important prehistoric and Viking-age artefacts, including finds from Jarlshof and St Ninian's Isle, as well as displays on maritime history, textiles and rural life.

Unst Heritage Centre, Norwick, Unst, Shetland.

EXCURSIONS

These are day-long excursions, chosen for the wide variety of monuments that they encompass; some involve using a car and others are best followed on foot (indicated on the maps as a broken line). Encouraged by Orkney Islands Council, several local community councils have produced useful leaflet guides to the natural and man-made environments of their individual islands.

Central and west mainland Orkney

From Stromness, take the A 965 towards Kirkwall; as the road swings eastwards along the south shore of the Loch of Stenness, the Bridge of Waithe spans the outflow from the loch into the sea, a stone bridge with three segmental arches built in 1859 to replace an earlier wooden bridge that consisted of logs laid across low stone piers (HY 281112). Almost immediately after the bridge is the signposted track to the fort and tomb at Unstan (no. 101). Continue on the A 965 to the mill at Tormiston (no. 30) and the great tomb of Maes Howe (no. 95).

Retrace your route along the main road, noting in a field on the right of the road the Barnhouse Stone, a magnificent slab standing over 3 m high (HY 312121), and take the B 9055 northwards to the henge and stone circle at Stenness (no. 84), to which the Barnhouse Stone may be related. The Stones of Stenness and the Ring of Brodgar (no. 83) should be appreciated together as a great ceremonial complex,

along with their outlying stones and burial mounds. Continue north-westwards along the B 9055, past the Ring of Bookan just visible as a circular earthwork in the field to the left (HY 283144), an unusual

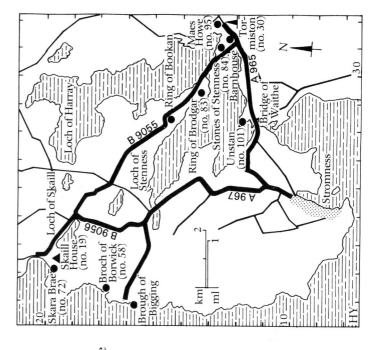

monument which may be another, smaller henge. At the Loch of Skaill, the road joins the B 9056 and skirts the north-east side of the loch to the carpark for Skara Brae on the Bay of Skaill (no. 72). Set back from the bay is the imposing 17th century Skaill House (no. 19).

From Skaill, follow the B 9056 south to the signposted turning for Yesnaby, an area of great natural beauty and considerable interest for geologists and botanists. The cliffs rise to a sheer height of some 30 m OD, and exposure to sea-spray has created a special environment for plants, suppressing the heather and encouraging plants such as crowberry, wild squill, sea pinks and wild thyme. A walk along the cliffs to the north allows a visit to the broch of Borwick (no. 58), while to the south there is a promontory fort, the Brough of Bigging (HY 218157), marked by two ramparts, about 30 m apart, across the neck of the promontory.

Eday and Calf of Eday, Orkney

The northern part of Eday, and the adjacent small island, Calf of Eday, are particularly interesting for their prehistoric archaeology; in contrast to the peat-covered landscape of today, Eday was in early prehistoric times a fertile and densely settled area, as the discovery of ancient field-boundaries beneath the blanket peat has demonstrated. The visitor arriving by sea at Backaland or by air at London should take a taxi (via the Eday co-operative to arrange a boat for the Calf) to just beyond Mill Loch (a Site of Special Scientific Interest on account of its breeding colony of Red-throated Divers) and begin this walking tour with the Stone of Setter (no. 86). This is one of the tallest single standing stones in the Northern Isles, and the effect of natural weathering has sculpted the sandstone into a very distinctively furrowed profile. Its location was very specifically designed to dominate the valleys to north and south, that to the north containing a number of chambered tombs and burial mounds,

and a remarkable, but undatable, stone enclosure. Walking north-westwards, much of the stonework of the chamber of Braeside tomb is visible (HY 563375), but little more than the entrance passage to the lower chamber may be seen of the two-storey tomb of Huntersquoy (HY 562377; cf no. 98). High above, on Vinquoy Hill (HY 99), is a well-preserved tomb that has recently been repaired and opened to the public by Orkney Islands Council.

Walk along the crest of the ridge northwards to the opening in the dyke before attempting to descend north-eastwards towards the shore of Calf Sound; skirt round Carrick House (no. 21), a 17th century house famous for its association with the capture of the pirate, John Gow, in 1725.

Continue south-eastwards along the road towards Calf Sound pier, and hire a boat across to the south-west

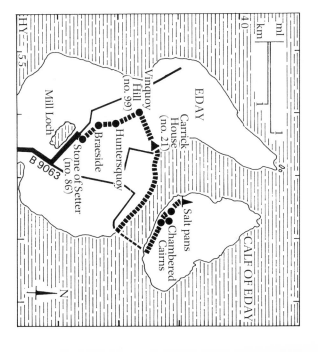

end of the Calf. This is a charming small island, now uninhabited, and a pleasant walk north-westwards encompasses not only well-preserved chambered tombs and the remains of an iron-age settlement but also a most unusual monument of industrial archaeology. Two of the tombs have small subterranean chambers and passages, dug into the hillside (HY 578386), which, though overgrown, may still be entered. Their oval chambers are divided by radial slabs into small burial compartments, and they appear originally to have been covered by low round cairns. A short distance further on along the coast is a larger composite tomb, which was entirely uncovered by excavation and left open so that the structure is quite clear (HY 578386). The long, roughly rectangular cairn lies across the contours of the slope and the entrance passage leading to the chamber lies at the uphill end—unlike the two subterranean tombs which face across Calf Sound. The long rectangular chamber is divided by pairs of tall upright slabs into four burial compartments: a partial human burial was found under a stone shelf in the innermost compartment and, surprisingly, two fine stone axes left on a ledge in the wall. This stalled chamber seems to have replaced an earlier two-compartment chamber which survives within the west end of the cairn. In later prehistoric times, a domestic settlement was established a little to the east of the cairn, but, although this too was excavated, it is now very overgrown.

Follow the shore northwards to see the ruins of a 17th century saltworks, an unusual industrial legacy and unique in the Northern Isles (HY 574391 and 575387). Both buildings were originally rectangular and lie end-on to the sea: the seaward gable was curved and stood in the sea, while the inland gable was cut into the slope of the land. A very thick wall divided the building into two, with a large fireplace on either side to evaporate the salt-water and dry the salt—the fireplace surviving in the south building has a rounded arch.

Papa Westray, Orkney

The island can be reached either by air or by sea from Kirkwall, and its monuments are best appreciated on foot, beginning at Holland in the centre of this fertile agricultural landscape (HY 488515). The placename Holland is common in the Northern Isles, in Shetland sometimes spelled houlland, and it means simply high land, from Old Norse *hó land*; here, as on North Ronaldsay, the name was given to the principal farm set on the highest part of the agricultural land.

The farm complex at Holland has several interesting features indicative of its status as the Traill estate farm, including a windmill base in a field in front of the house (HY 489512), a smithy, a lectern-type dovecote, a corn-drying kiln and, unusually for the Northern Isles, a horse-engine house. Horse-powered threshing machinery was normally in the open air, but this is a well-built covered horse-gang, a circular structure with a conical flagstone roof (the original spaces between its wall-sections have been built up); the machinery has gone, but originally the horses were harnessed to wooden poles attached to a geared wheel, which turned a shaft running from the horse-shed into the adjacent barn to the threshing machinery. In a small enclosure to the south of the farm buildings are the circular stone bases for haystacks, the stones for each base being neatly gathered into a small cairn between times when the old hay is finished and the new has yet to be stacked. Before leaving the farm, arrange with the owner for a boat-trip to the Holm of Papay later in the day. This can also be arranged through the Papay Community Co-operative at Beltane House, a short distance along the road east of Holland, where a row of farmworkers' cottages has been excellently converted into a shop and guest-house.

From Holland, take the signposted track westwards past the dovecote to the neolithic houses on the shore at Knap of Howar (no. 73), their turf-covered walls often bright with sea-pinks.

From here it is a pleasant walk northwards along the shore to Munkerhoose, the site of a broch with external buildings which is under severe erosion by the sea (stonework is visible in the cliff), and the church of St Boniface (HY 488526). This church was built in the 12th century as a rectangular nave and chancel, the nave having been extended westwards in the early 18th century in order to insert a loft for the Traill family and the chancel at some period demolished and its site used as the Traill family burial enclosure. Two Early Christian cross-incised gravestones have been found buried in the churchyard (one in RMS and the other in THM), indicating that there was ecclesiastical activity on the site even before the construction of the 12th century church. Contemporary with the latter is a Norse hogback tombstone (no. 54) still to be seen (though in summer it may be overgrown) in the churchyard on the east side of the church.

Follow the track from the church to the main road and return north and almost immediately east along a track to the east shore of the island; walking southwards along the shore you will pass a typical farm mound at Mayback (HY 495524), betraying the centuries over which a single place may be occupied, and a row of seven boat nausts at Skennist (HY 496519), before reaching the pier and the boat for the Holm.

The tiny island is now the home for sheep and a colony of black guillemots, but its archaeology is eloquent witness to former glory in human eyes as well, for there are no fewer than three neolithic chambered tombs. Looking like a grass-covered submarine at the south end is a hugely extravagant Maes Howe type of tomb (no. 92), into which the visitor descends by ladder through the conning tower, at the north end the outlines of a recently excavated stalled cairn (see under no. 92), while between the two may be discerned the surface traces of the third tomb, probably another stalled cairn (HY 507518). The shell

of a building on the west shore was a stable for the ponies formerly kept on the island.

Back on Papay, follow the track southwards to the old corn-mill at Hookin (HY 500512), astride a burn running from the Loch of St Tredwell to the sea. There was once a fine chapel to the Pictish saint, Triduana, on a promontory projecting into the loch on its east side, but little remains to be seen of what was a favourite place of pilgrimage in late medieval times (HY 496508). Between the loch and the Bay of Burland

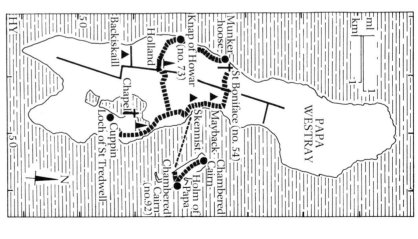

is a well-preserved section of the treb dyke which used to divide the island into two unequal parts (HY 496506-499505), surviving as a broad bank, almost a metre high. Traces of the western section of the dyke may be seen near Backiskaill, where there is also an excellent example of a crescentic burnt mound (HY 485509).

Rousay

The ferries from Tingwall and Kirkwall come in at Trumland pier in Wyre Sound on the south-east shore of the island and, although it is possible to cover this entire excursion on foot, a more leisurely day will be achieved by taking the mini-bus or a taxi from the pier to Midhowe. Rousay has a great wealth of archaeological monuments: at least twelve chambered cairns, many cairns, barrows and burnt mounds, eight brochs, an important Viking-age settlement and cemetery at Westness, and a fascinating pre-improvement agricultural landscape at Quandale. The fact that so many prehistoric monuments have been excavated and made accessible and comprehensible to the public is primarily a reflection of the energy and financial generosity of Walter Grant, who lived in Trumland House and was responsible for many

excavations in the 1930s. The upland interior of the island rises unusually high for Orkney (250 m OD), and the fertile areas lie along the coast, determining the distribution of both modern and prehistoric settlement.

From the road above Midhowe, follow the signposted path downhill towards the sea—there is a wonderful view across Eynhallow Sound—and enter the unlikely looking hangar to see the chambered tomb of Midhowe (no. 96) as revealed by excavation. A little to the north-west close to the shore, stands the broch and its outworks (no. 60); the name Midhowe originally distinguished this broch-mound from one to the north-west (North Howe, HY 370307) and another to the south-east (South Howe, HY 372303), both of which are still visible, though the latter is badly eroded by the sea.

Follow the shore southwards to the ruins of the post-Reformation church of St Mary's (the great buttresses were added to the ruin at the end of the 19th century in an attempt to halt its decay), and, at one corner of the churchyard, the foundations of an earlier medieval square stone tower (HY 373301), known as The Wirk. Further south along the shore towards Westness, there are the overgrown remains of another stalled cairn, Knowe of Rowiegar (HY 373297), very similar to Midhowe. Continuing along the shore, notice traces of excavations on the site of an important Viking-age farm (HY 375296) with its adjacent cemetery on the low headland of Moa Ness and boat-naust on the south side of the headland.

Sheltered amongst trees is Westness House (HY 383289), built around 1750 and only supplanted as the grand house of the Rousay estate when Trumland House was built. Walk up the track to the road and continue south-eastwards along the road for almost 2 km. On the natural terraces above the road is an important group of neolithic chambered cairns; Knowe of Lairo (HY 398279) is a long cairn in which a

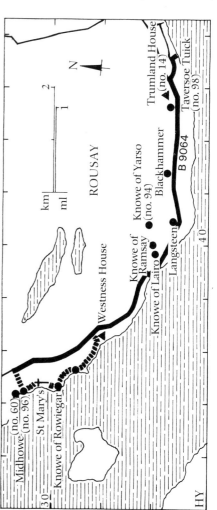

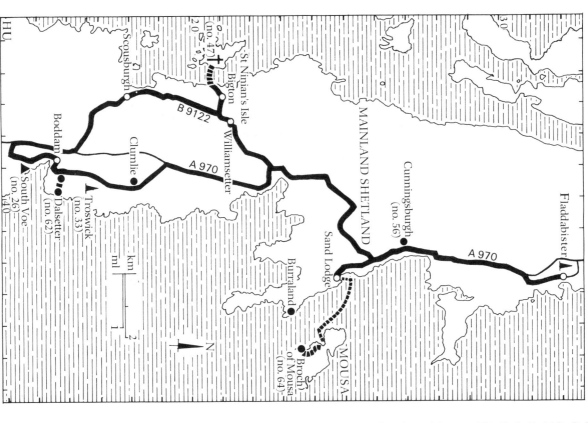

small burial chamber was enclosed at the east end of a cairn almost 50 m long, piled high over the chamber and then tailing away to a low north-west end; the Knowe of Ramsay (HY 400279) was originally a magnificent tomb like Midhowe with fourteen burial compartments but it survives as little more than a low mound; high above is the Knowe of Yarso (no. 94), given an artificial roof after excavation and well worth the climb–as is the view from its vantage point of 100 m OD.

Beside the road is an impressive standing stone about 2.2 m high, known as thé Langsteen (HY 404274), and along the road to the east are the signposted and well-preserved tombs of Blackhammer (HY 414276) and Taversoe Tuick (no. 98), excavated, as were all the tombs in this excursion, by Walter Grant and his colleagues. A fitting end to the day would be a glimpse of Grant's home, Trumland House (no. 14).

Southern mainland Shetland

This excursion is designed to sample the range of monuments south of Lerwick, but it does not include sites within Lerwick, the multi-period site at Jarlshof on the Sumburgh peninsula (no. 55), or the forts on the Scatness peninsula (no. 66), all of which are very absorbing and require a half-day each. Take the A 970 south from Lerwick for almost 10 km, and turn off to the left for Fladdabister, a village with an archaic character and good examples of lime kilns (HU 437321). After rejoining the main road south of the village, continue to Cunningsburgh to see the prehistoric and Viking-age steatite quarries (no. 56). About 1 km further on, take the side-road on the left signposted for Sand Lodge and the Mousa ferry (see no. 64 for both Sand Lodge and Mousa) and, en route across Mousa Sound, try to distinguish the broch of Burraland on the coast south of Sand Lodge (HU 446232).

Returning to the A 970, continue south to HU 399226, where the B 9122 branches off to the right; the old

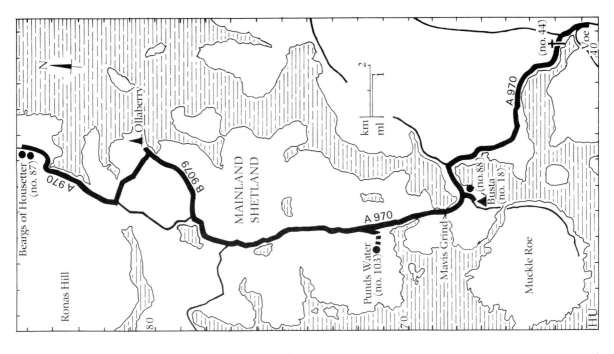

village of Williamsetter retains some thatched buildings, and a side-road west to Bigton allows a pleasant walk across the sand to St Ninian's Isle (no. 47). The B road joins up with the A 970 in time to take a signposted minor road to the croft museum at South Voe (no. 26). Turn north again, and follow the coast road through Boddam to see the neolithic houses and broch at Dalsetter (no. 62), the click mills on the Clumlie burn above Troswick (no. 33) and the broch incorporated into the steading at Clumlie (HU 404181), finally rejoining the A 970.

Northern mainland Shetland

Starting at Voe, some 30 km north of Lerwick on the A 970, visit the old church overlooking Olna Firth (no. 44) before continuing to Brae. Beyond the village, turn south on a minor road along the west side of Busta Voe to see the massive standing stone (no. 88) and the enchanting old house at Busta (no. 18). Returning to the A 970, continue northwards over the narrow Mavis Grind, somewhat romantically regarded as separating the Atlantic from the North Sea, and visit the well-preserved neolithic tomb of Punds Water (no. 103). North again, the B 9079 leads off to the north-east to the fishing station of Ollaberry with its fine 19th century pier and post-crane, and, in the graveyard of the modern church, a grandiose 18th century funerary memorial apparently attached to the rubble gable of the earlier church. A minor road leads from Ollaberry north-westwards to rejoin the A 970 and, about 5 km further north, the remarkable tableau of Beorgs of Housetter with its standing stones and cairns (no. 87). The wild landscape of Northmavine is dominated by Ronas Hill, 450 m OD, a steep-sided hill whose summit is usually wreathed in mist and yet bears a neolithic tomb (HU 305834)—one can only marvel at the effort and idealism of its builders.

Whalsay, Shetland

The island of Whalsay presents a most interesting microcosm of Shetland history and environment, most of which can be appreciated within a day. The island has been inhabited since the early days of human settlement in Shetland, and its prehistoric monuments together with unique later survivals of Hanseatic trade are among the most remarkable of Shetland's man-made heritage.

The passenger and car ferry from Laxo Voe on the adjacent mainland (reached from Lerwick via the A 970 and the B 9071) docks at Symbister, a harbour used by Hanseatic merchants in the 16th and 17th centuries who built trading booths and storehouses (no. 9). Take the road northwards along the west side of the island to see the cup-marked rocks at Brough (no. 82). Below Brough the lighthouse on Suther Ness guards the entrance into Linga Sound (HU 550653), while the adjacent Kirk Ness (both are virtually islands joined to the mainland by narrow isthmuses) is so-called because the existing church stands on the site of an early medieval church, recalling the location of St Ninian's Isle church (no. 47). A platform in the churchyard may mark the position of the earlier church.

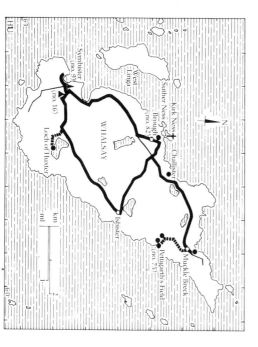

Continue north-eastwards towards the road end at Skaw; a good example of a burnt mound may be seen from the road at Challister (HU 565655), and, again from the road, a standing stone in a somewhat odd location close to the shore of Skaw Voe (HU 589664).

The easiest way to reach the remarkable neolithic structures above Yoxie Geo is probably to follow the peat track from Muckle Breck (HU 587660) south-westwards past planticrues into the moorland to the chambered tomb known as Pettigarths Field (no. 75), with its commanding view of the ancient settlement area below (the Benie Hoose is hidden in a dip of the land). An alternative route offering magnificent views of the steep cliffs and geos is to walk from the road end at Skaw (HU 594666) southwards alongside the airstrip and then follow the coast to Yoxie Geo.

Return to the cross-roads at Brough and turn left via Isbister towards the Loch of Huxter: the interior of the island is almost entirely peat-covered, governing the distribution of modern settlement and still providing an invaluable source of fuel. Between Isbister and Nuckro Water there is a fine series of planticrues to the right of the road. A track leads down from the road to the west shore of the Loch of Huxter, whence a very wet and boggy walk over old peat banks round the south shore will lead to the islet fort (HU 558620; only in a dry season should the visitor attempt to cross to the fort along its rocky causeway), but it can also be viewed distantly from the road. The tiny islet in its naturally defensive position is linked to the shore by a narrow man-made causeway of rubble, and almost the entire area of the islet is enclosed by an irregularly shaped wall, incorporating on its landward side the remains of a massive blockhouse or fortified gateway. Much stone has been robbed from the fort to build planticrues on the adjacent shore.

Continuing west to Symbister, visit the fine Georgian house (no. 16) before returning to the harbour.

BIBLIOGRAPHY

Aslet, C   *The Last Country Houses*, New Haven & London, 1982.

Baldwin, JR (ed)   *Scandinavian Shetland: an ongoing tradition?* Edinburgh, 1978.

Cant, RG   *The Medieval Churches and Chapels of Shetland*, Lerwick, 1975.

Clouston, JS   *A History of Orkney*, Kirkwall, 1932.

Cruden, S   *The Scottish Castle*, Edinburgh, 1960.

Donaldson, G   *Shetland Life under Earl Patrick*, Edinburgh, 1958.

Dunbar, JG   *The Historic Architecture of Scotland*, London, 2nd edition 1978.

Fawcett, R   *Scottish Medieval Churches*, Edinburgh, 1985.

Fenton, A   *The Northern Isles: Orkney and Shetland*, Edinburgh, 1978.

Fenton, A & Palsson, H (eds)   *The Northern and Western Isles in the Viking World*, Edinburgh, 1984.

Fojut, N   *A Guide to Prehistoric Shetland*, Lerwick, 1981.

Hedges, J   *Tomb of the Eagles*, London, 1984.

Hedges, JW   *A Guide to Isbister Chambered Tomb and Liddle Burnt Mound, South Ronaldsay, Orkney*, Oxford, 1985.

Henshall, AS   *The Chambered Tombs of Scotland*, Edinburgh, 2 vols, 1963 & 1972.

Hume, JR   *The Industrial Monuments of Scotland, 2 The Highlands & Islands*, London, 1977.

Miller, R   *Orkney*, London, 1976.

Munro, RW   *Scottish Lighthouses*, Stornoway, 1979.

Nicolson, JR   *Shetland*, Newton Abbot, 1972.

Nicolson, JR   *Lerwick Harbour*, Lerwick, 1976.

Orkney Heritage, vol. 2, Birsay: a centre of political and ecclesiastical power, Kirkwall, 1983.

Pálsson, H & Edwards, P   Orkneyinga Saga, London, 1978.

Renfrew, C (ed)   The Prehistory of Orkney, Edinburgh, 1985.

Ritchie, A & Ritchie, G   The Ancient Monuments of Orkney, Edinburgh, 1978.

Ritchie, G & Ritchie, A   Scotland: Archaeology and Early History, London, 1981.

Royal Commission on the Ancient and Historical Monuments of Scotland,   An Inventory of the Ancient and Historical Monuments of Orkney and Shetland, Edinburgh, 1946.

Wainwright, FT (ed)   The Northern Isles, London, 1962.

Waterston, G & Jones, J   Fair Isle: A Photographic History, 1983.

Withrington, DJ (ed)   Shetland and the Outside World 1469-1969, Aberdeen, 1983.

There are also guide booklets or leaflets to individual monuments in the care of Historic Buildings and Monuments, published by HMSO, Edinburgh: Brough of Birsay, Doumby Click Mill, Jarlshof, the Earl's and Bishop's Palaces in Kirkwall, Maes Howe, Mousa and Clickhimin, Noltland Castle, Scalloway Castle and Skara Brae.

INDEX

Printed in Scotland by (3803)
Dd. 0287759 C15 7/93